What Have You Carried Over?
Poems of 42 Days and Other Works

1077	Eser: What Have You Carried Over? Yazar: Gülten Akın Yayıncı: Talisman House Publishers Ülke: ABD

GÜLTEN AKIN

WHAT HAVE YOU CARRIED OVER?
POEMS OF 42 DAYS AND OTHER
WORKS

EDITED BY
SALIHA PAKER AND MEL KENNE

Talisman House, Publishers • 2014
Greenfield, Massachusetts

Manufactured in the United States of America
Printed on acid-free paper

14 15 7 6 5 4 3 2 1 FIRST EDITION

Book designed by Samuel Retsov

Published in the United States of America by
Talisman House, Publishers
P.O. Box 896
Greenfield, Massachusetts 01302

Grateful acknowledgment is made for the generous support given to
the publication of this book by the Turkish Ministry of Culture.

ISBN: 978-1-58498-096-4

ACKNOWLEDGEMENTS:

The editors extend their warmest thanks to Gülten Akın not only for granting us the great privilege of compiling a book of her work but for being so generous with her time and tireless in offering vital help in the task of translating and presenting it. Our gratitude also goes to the publishers, estate managers and family members who gave their permission for the translations in this collection to be published or republished: Osman Streater (for Nermin Menemencioğlu's translations in her *Penguin Book of Turkish Verse*); Ann Fielder and Özgür Yalım (for the translations done by Özcan Yalım, William A. Fielder and Dionis C. Riggs), and David Perlman (The Rockingham Press, for translations by Ruth Christie in *Modern Turkish Poetry*). Great thanks are due, of course, to the dedicated translators whose work appears herein: Nermin Menemencioğlu, Talat S. Halman, Önder Otçu, and the participants of the Cunda Workshop for Translators of Turkish Literature, including those whose translations we've used: Ruth Christie, Cemal Demircioğlu, Arzu Eker Roditakis, İpek Seyalioğlu, and Sidney Wade. We are grateful as well to Zeynep Uzunbay for her judicious help and guidance in sharing her scholarly research on Gülten Akın's poetry with us. We thank Akif Elbistan of Cihan News Agency for providing the cover photo. Finally, we wish to express our great thanks to the Turkish Ministry of Culture and the TEDA program for their vital support of this and other translation projects, and to Ed Foster for his unstinting dedication to the publication of Turkish poetry through Talisman House, Publishers, and *Talisman Magazine*.

Contents:

Introduction by Saliha Paker ... i

Saliha Paker

INTRODUCTION

In a poll conducted by the long-standing *Milliyet* Arts Journal in 2008, Gülten Akın (1933-) was voted the "greatest living Turkish poet" by an outstanding majority of Turkey's writers, poets, and literary critics. In the same year, she was awarded the prestigious Erdal Öz Literature Prize "for her life-long dedication to the art of poetry, for the remarkable innovative turn in her recent work, all of which reflect the quality achieved in the contemporary Turkish poetic tradition.". Gülten Akın's poems and prose criticism have inspired very many poets, men as well as women. Very few would disagree with the following description of her poetry by an anonymous contributor to a popular blog (Ekşi Sözlük) in Turkey: "Gülten Akın knew how to pull together the energy of socially conscious poetry, the rich imagery of the Second New Movement and the sensitivity of womanhood. She is the true mother of Turkish poetry" (2002).

Winner of many awards since she started publishing in the 1950s, Gülten Akın has often pointed out that her poetry is bound up with the immediate experiences of her life, but memory and its questionings also play an important role in it. "Garden Vines" (2007), for instance, is a special reckoning with memory, and the title of our book is taken from its refrain: "from those days to these / what have you carried over / what have I?" These lines ring with both a personal and a social sense of responsibility. Among the memories recalled in this poem, a rather painful one stands out from the time of the second military coup (1971) in Turkey: "Up against the Ziverbey mansion / a house, Istanbul / between roses and screams / I must've been blind, blinded I was then / Outside the sun shone past us." It was discovered later that the so-called "mansion," next to which she had happened to live for some months, was in fact a house of interrogation under torture.

Gülten Akın's work spans sixty years of often turbulent change in the society and politics of her country, marked dramatically by three military coups in 1960, 1971, and 1980. It reflects both the frustrating conflicts and the quiet moments of her private life as a wife and mother of five, but also her unwavering commitment towards upholding social conscience as a universal value against injustice and inequality. Her deeply ingrained Sûfî beliefs surface too, especially in her later poems. In this selection of Gülten Akın's work, the first to be published in English, the reader will find translations that represent only some of the poems in twelve of her major collections. *Poems of 42 Days* is translated in its entirety and holds a central place in this volume, as it does in her Turkish corpus of poetry. Hilal Sürsal's book, *Voice of Hope. Turkish Woman Poet Gülten Akın*, which was published by Indiana University in 2008, is a comprehensive study of the poet's work, containing a wide range of translations, mostly in excerpt.

Gülten Akın was the first woman to achieve unequivocal prominence as a poet in the literary establishment of the sixties and seventies. She is often named among the poets of the revolutionary movement known as the "Second New," but, as she herself has testified (in a personal communication), she never identified personally with this movement; in fact she has criticized its overemphasis on imagery at the expense of meaning. She had already made a name for herself with her first collection, *Hour of the Wind*, which was published in 1956, when she was 23, and awarded the Varlık prize; this was also the year she got her degree in Law from Ankara University and married Yaşar Cankoçak, a graduate of the School of Political Science of the same University.

The publication of her second collection, *I Cut my Black Black Hair*, in 1960, coincided with the first military coup, which paradoxically introduced greater freedom of expression, especially for the left. This collection brought her even greater popularity; its title poem must be the first to herald the women's liberation movement in Turkey. The collection that followed it in 1964, *In the Shallows*, was awarded the prestigious prize of the Turkish Language Society, for its excellence in the poetic use of modern Turkish. In these early poems, Akın was sharply critical, uncompromising, and unsentimental in the probing of her world. However, in the opinion of Memet Fuat (1985), a widely influential left-wing critic and editor, she was not "in the vanguard" until "she made a sudden breakthrough in the 1970s; turning towards social issues and reflecting the suffering brought about by conflicts in the country, she wrote with a modern perception of the traditional Anatolian popular epic, elegy and song, and spoke out for resistance to brute force and oppression. Her poems gave voice to the constructive anger of woman's sensitivity, and of motherhood." These words show how she was perceived by the dominant literary left and, most probably, why in 1985 she was included as the only woman among 82 poets in Memet Fuat's major anthology of contemporary Turkish poetry *Çağdaş Türk Şiiri Antolojisi*.

As Gülten Akın made clear in an article she wrote in 1977, she never put much weight on what

> for hundreds of years... men have set apart as "female sensitivity" and blown out of proportion. What they mean by it is nothing but the ability to sympathize with others. Hence it's a passive function... If women have an equal share in the burden of eliminating the primary contradictions of the world, -- and that's what's happening now-- we will speak of a human sensitivity which is not held exclusive to women. "Women's sensitivity" is a decrepit concept that does not belong to this age; the creative powers of women should not be inflated and isolated from art and creativity in general, like some anomaly... Sensitivity of the kind reserved "for women" and nurtured, under special care, is bound to dry up. (Akın 1977/2001)

In her own words, Gülten Akın was "born in the tenth year of the modern Turkish republic and was raised in an environment that sought a modern outlook but was accustomed to pursuing the traditional way of life." She belonged to a large traditional, patriarchal family of venerable elders of the faith in the small Anatolian town of Yozgat. As the eldest of three sisters and a smart student, she was brought up by her father to compete against men, while also kept aware of being "a girl," that her freedom was restricted to

> trying to come first as a racehorse. If I got bad grades, I was consoled. My honor was kept alive, but I could sense the expectation. It was terrible.... Yet poets were revered in our household and poetry was part of our everyday life and language. On long winter nights, my grandfather would recite and chant verse narratives about the life of the Prophet, and we listened to him for hours. My uncles both on my mother's and father's side wrote poetry, and I used to rummage through their suitcases in the attic for books of all kinds, which I read avidly. Russian classics, Nazım Hikmet, Sabahattin Ali, poetry anthologies. (Akın 1988/2001)

Gülten Akın has described the main stages in her life in the long poem "Summer" (1971); she also has discussed them in the talk she gave in 2006 at the Cunda International Workshop for Translators of Turkish Literature:

After ten years of a happy childhood, the winds of World War II and its aftermath of hardships drove us, with our families, to the big cities. It was traumatic for me to move away from wide spaces and try to fit in narrow ones, and to have to make do with less, to witness unfairness and injustice in human relationships. The feeling that everything was alien transformed

iv

me from an extroverted, cheerful, easygoing child into an introverted adolescent. That was when I felt literally in the underworld. Then I wrote a poem. And it was poetry that saved me....

At first, I was preoccupied with my own problems, which seemed to be at the center of everything I knew. I couldn't help it. The sudden encounter with new things in life and the difficulty in adapting led me to write introspectively about myself. Then, after a while, it was back to the provinces, back to my blurred Anatolian childhood. I became re-acquainted with the people, their language, their ways of life. As a family, we lived in many different towns, central or remote, in Anatolia, for short periods. On account of my husband's work as a government administrator, we were appointed to some, while we were sort of exiled to others. My husband was somewhat headstrong about his own ideas and policies as an administrator, and I was writing poetry. As you know, poetry too makes people feel on edge. Because of that, we never got to live anywhere for more than two years; we moved about a lot, which proved to be all to my advantage. I worked as a school teacher and sometimes also as a lawyer, mixing with all kinds of people from all walks of life, acquiring priceless tools for my poetry. As a result my poems changed. They came to be more about life as I experienced it with and among other people. I felt that I had an entire gamut of social themes at my finger tips. (Akın 2006/2013)

Gülten Akın describes her earlier poems as having "embraced a wide field of references that were only indirectly connected" (Ibid.). An example from this period is the poem, "Who What" (1956), with the telling refrain "Let who will save what be guessed / Yes, but not known."

v

In the course of her half-nomadic life (1958-1972) in many different parts of the country, her close relationship with people living in villages and in small towns, drove her to write "poems (which I) imagined as arrows that would make an impact with a direct hit" (Ibid.). This was the first shift in her poetics, as represented by *The Red Carnation* (1971), which foregrounded her association with socialist thinking. However, she has always believed that ideology must never constrain the aesthetic quality of the poem. "A poet's ideology is like the sap of a tree, which cannot be seen but only imagined. If it has to be integrated in poetry, that must be achieved without doing the slightest damage to the aesthetic quality" (Ibid.).

A fine example from The Red Carnation is the poem "Spring," embedded in popular memory with its first two lines: "Oh, no one's got the time / to stop'n think about fine things...". A more elusive one is "Anatolian Ellas and the Statues," in which the clash between tradition and modernity is implicit.

In 1972, it was back to Ankara, a year after the second military coup, followed by a worsening of the political situation that was capped by yet another coup in 1980, which brought with it even more gruelling years. Gülten Akın worked for the Turkish Language Society, the Ministry of Culture, and the Human Rights Association, of which she was a founder; she describes this period in her life, especially from 1978 onwards, as "a heavy, very heavy one, under intense oppression. Our family got its share of imprisonment for eight years" (Akın 1988/2001). The powerful and poignant *Poems of 42 Days* (1986) is her personal testimony of this period, especially of the traumatic experiences that involved her son, many other young political prisoners on a hunger strike, and their families. This collection of alternating lyric and prose poems focuses mostly on mothers, from many parts of the country, from all walks of life. "It was not just a personal suffering, but one that we shared with others" (Akın 2006/2013). *Poems of 42 Days* must, in truth, be read as an epic of human dignity and resilience against modern-day cruelty and injustice.

"Poets who draw out their poems from life write about their life experience," said Gülten Akın (1988/2001). Her *Laments and Songs* (1976) and *Hymns* (1983) also belong to this deeply painful period that found voice in lines such as,"A fret-saw in my heart / round and round I pace on a burning stone." But Gülten Akın has also pointed out that she "never lost hope, never let my sufferings crush it. I kept it alive but hidden in my poems..." (Akın 1988/2001).

Many years later, in 1995, her collection, *Then I Grew Old* appeared, well-known for its title poem of two lines: " — Then I grew old, behold / A sentence as long as a novel." It summed up not only the exhaustion of years past but marked the end of a phase in her poetics. Far from diminishing in strength, the poems that followed in the next two decades were driven with the fresh energy of a quieter but still questioning life. "In my most recent books," she said," I've tried to bring in the indirectness, the multiple connotations of my earlier style to merge with a certain directness that has sunk in deeper. Now, I'm happier with myself." Most of the older themes continued to reverberate in a different, sometimes Sûfî, context, as in the case of "Two-Way Gipsy;" and "the crazy girl" of the early poems would become the "crazy queen" who, in "The Cloak," said, "On my own shoulders I placed the cloak of self-censure." Explaining this spiritual aspect of her poetry, Gülten Akın has said:

> Sûfî beliefs are in my roots... I never felt divided by the double perception of tradition and modernity. On the contrary, they nurtured each other, and this was my greatest advantage. Knowing about modernity and benefiting from it, I was able to ingest the traditional. The Sûfî tradition has always remained a fundamental part of me, and my poetry has nothing to do with what is now a fashionable literary trend. (Akın 2006/2013)

As translators of Gülten Akın, we first met her in 2006, at the initial meeting of the Cunda International Workshop for Translators of Turkish Literature. She was invited to talk about her life and poetry, from which I have quoted above. We began with "I Cut My Black Black Hair" and "Two-Way Gypsy," and decided to go on translating Gülten Akın's poetry for a special publication project. In the years that followed, several of the translations were done with more than two collaborators, some of whom were poets. *Poems of 42 Days* remained as the central piece; some of them were presented for discussion at the 2009 Workshop, and we were warmly encouraged to continue. The translation was finished in the summer of 2012, by which time many more poems were included for a fuller selection. We welcomed some very fine translations given to us by Gülten Akın, which were done in the 1970s and 1980s by her friends, the distinguished translators Nermin Menemcioğlu, Talat S. Halman, and Özcan Yalım, who had collaborated with the American poet Dionis C. Riggs and William Fielder in Ankara, and a later translation by Önder Otçu. Sometimes it was difficult to choose from the vast range of poems composed over six decades. For instance, we could not include any from The Epic of Maraş and Ökkeş (1972) and the Epic of Seyran (1979), both awarded prizes in the 1970s. In September 2012, at our seventh annual Workshop, we celebrated the end of the translation process in the presence of Gülten Akın, who gave us her blessing.

In the course of our long journey through the poems of Gülten Akın, Mel Kenne and I were particularly mindful of not interfering with the poet's syntax, lineation and punctuation, unless we felt it was necessary. For example, in "I Cut My Black Black Hair," our first translation from Gülten Akın, we experimented with staggering the original lines for a visual expansion to reinforce the spirit of freedom which the poem celebrates. We wanted the voice of our translations to remain in close kinship to the poet's Turkish, to the impact of rhythm and, whenever possible, of rhyme, despite the difficulty of rendering all these in a language so very different from the original one. I believe this could only be done effectively with the touch of a masterful poet who respects the original poet's style. I am therefore deeply thankful to Mel Kenne, himself a poet, for his wholehearted dedication to Gülten Akın's poetry. Akın's diction is rooted in the Turkish vernacular, sometimes dialectal, but her syntax, often elliptic, is complex, and connections between reference points can sometimes be obscure. In such instances, Gülten Akın graciously responded to our queries, for which we are extremely grateful.

What better way to conclude than with Gülten Akın's own words from a speech she gave in 1994:

> Poetry is nuclear energy squeezed into lines. Something that will explode into particles. This is what frightens the established order and those who are in charge of it. Poetry is pleasure and profoundness, infinite independence and freedom from ties, a very fine balance, an inner order. Patience and passion.
>
> I can't think of a world without poetry. For everyone. (Akın 1994/2001)

REFERENCES:

Akın, Gülten (2006/2013), "Gülten Akın on Poetry, Ideology and Conscience" (trans. Saliha Paker)., in *Aeolian Visions / Versions: Modern Classics and New Writing from Turkey, from The Cunda International Workshop for Translators of Turkish Literature, 2006-2012*, eds. Mel Kenne, Saliha Paker, Amy Spangler. London: Milet Publishing Ltd. Forthcoming in 2013.
— —(1994/2001) "İnce Şeyleri Anlamak" (Understanding Fine Things) in *Şiiri Düzde Kuşatmak* (Embracing Poetry in Plain Prose), Istanbul: Yapı Kredi Yayınları.
— —(1988/2001) "Acıya Yenik Değiliz, Ne Ben, Ne de Şiirim" (Pain Has Not Defeated Us. Neither Me nor My Poetry. Interview with Zeynep Oral) in

Şiiri Düzde Kuşatmak (Embracing Poetry in Plain Prose), Istanbul: Yapı Kredi
Yayınları.

—— (1977/2001) "Kadın Yaratıcılığında, İnsanca Duyarlığa Evet" (Affirming
Human Sensitivity in Women's Creativity) in *Şiiri Düzde Kuşatmak* (Embrac-
ing Poetry in Plain Prose), Istanbul: Yapı Kredi Yayınları.

Fuat, Memet (1985) Ed. *Çağdaş Türk Şiiri Antolojisi* (Anthology of Contemporary
Turkish Poetry), Istanbul: Adam.

Sürsal, Hilal (2008) *Voice of Hope. Turkish Woman Poet Gülten Akın*, Bloomington:
Indiana University.

from *The Hour of Wind* (1956)

NIGHT OF THE LOST

Now the world is slowing in the sky
You are far from all living beings, you are alone.
The wind has tired of the summits
The mountain flowers have fallen asleep
The moon has passed beyond the chimney
                              Won't you sleep?

A damp chill has passed through the black street
All day long something crackled
Beneath your feet
All day long you were silent as the dead
If you had but known the other side is lighted
You would have burned your old poems
You would have rejoiced inwardly
At a pinch of cloud and two drops of rain
If you had known that the other side is lighted.

This is not your normal state
To lose all strength
This is not your normal state
To lose life itself.

Turned toward you with his most human face
For this day, is the one you call friend.
Forget the distance
Wake him up, untimely though it is,
And bring him to your side.

Translated by Özcan Yalım, William C. Fielder and Dionis C. Riggs

THE HOUR OF WIND

You, man, the meadow and grass
You water and trim this way from day one
By day three will have grown back again
You, man, these sparrows you scare off
at mid-morning—just to be doing something—
They'll have forgotten it by evening

The fine point of my hurt
Behind my eyes will keep growing

My mind in whistles and tunes
In the windy hours I can't keep it home
Gusting or not, it's out in the streets
Can't hold it home in the hours of wind
Like tramps the streets
Filling my memories

Dreariness from top to toe
What is it to recall what's memory
Just far away from this city, this park
Wherever it may be

The meadows and sparrows are, as I am, tired
How to carry my hands now
On the roof, on the eaves, on the chimney
Swings a sleeping blueness swings

You, man, what you water and trim
It's neither grass nor meadow but another thing
Something held within your pruning shears in your water
It's what you go on thinking and thinking
—May I die if this is mindreading or knowing
It's as clear as day—
That's your Allah and your Satan.

Translated by Saliha Paker and Mel Kenne

2

SONG OF THE CRAZY GIRL III

If on one of the big streets I met you
if reaching out my hand I held you took you away
if I looked into your eyes, your eyes, if we never spoke
if you understood

If I reached out my hand, if I couldn't hold
all the love I held within, if I thought
of all that loneliness, no, if I didn't
if you never suspected it
you would never suspect it anyway
that song would start and stop all on its own

rain falls, the acacias are dripping
at night clouds fly about
I'm crazy about rain, crazy about the cloud
what you look at as living is a big game
either love me or kill me

on one of those wide roads you've got to lose everything
start all over again like insects
in this Godless darkness, resisting the rain
burn O heart of your own strangeness burn
what's gone is gone

Translated by Saliha Paker and Mel Kenne

DYING–LIVING

Somebody was weeping for me
For the first time they held me up
Nobody should hear this except you
I must not have known how to live

By the pine grove I washed my hands at the spring
My loved one left me, was gone, was no good
The lock of hair I held, I left to the wind
My hands were as warm as if I'd held his
Now all who are alive are far away from me
Now all my senses are in denial
As if I'd never felt never seen never loved

A woman in black so young and fresh
A child opened his big eyes and laughed
On me three green leaves of the bitterest hue
That's how in that final moment I sensed the pleasure of living
From top to toe
Suppose if you can that I'm not dead.

Translated by Saliha Paker and Mel Kenne

FORGIVE AND FOREGO

In streets that are awake
It's clear to me from your footsteps
You're my destiny

Each person has a song preceding each self,
Sung as soon as each is born to the world

If by a wild swallow's wing
My fingers go crazy with pleasure
I won't have it, it's not you

On the final return to the same fairytale
The one you're waiting for in the same mood
Will or will not be loved to death
In the strange whiteness of the nights

To you I'm leaving my dreams
Siblings to small sins
Just forgive and forego

Translated by Saliha Paker and Mel Kenne

FEMININE

… Who can say in which latitude
It's now raining on dry lands
For how many nights in the middle of a film
You reach out and grasp my hand

For some reason each time you take my hand
Each time you hold my hand just once
Then with all my cases, my causes, I'm out there
On my own then with the whole crowd within me

Between air and sea
Between bread and peace
You're all there believe me
For an infinite number of things, for instance
For things that got broken or fell apart
So many times you deceived yourself

The mountains can stay as high as they like
I cannot keep you out of my sight, stay
Living with small deceptions is good
Take death away

Translated by Saliha Paker and Mel Kenne

CAPRICIOUS

On the other side of visible things you're there
Darkness has grown so large don't ask, return
Even if we have to live as insects and weeds
Don't ask, just return

This sky must withdraw from above us
These nights that are still, motionless
In long and hopeless concepts
The mountains and houses of this world must withdraw

The one whose stars are larger than the mountain must understand
The one who floods the rivers must understand
Must shed light on your hands, I can't make them out
The light must stop great waters must stop
The one in possession of the stars must stop
Don't ask, just return

It's clear, such quiet effort is in vain
The leaf will exhaust its green, the song will age
Surely there'll be one who forgets, one who awaits
Don't ask, just return

These evenings exposed to the wind
In the palm of my hand forever my heart
Don't ask, just return

Translated by Saliha Paker and Mel Kenne

from *I Cut my Black Black Hair* (1960)

I CUT MY BLACK BLACK HAIR

It was far away   turn

                it was close   turn

                                it was all around   turn

Taboo

      law

              custom   turn

Inside

              outside

                      beside me   I'm not

Inside me   shame

                    Outside me   work

                          My left side   love

How could this   be life   turn

Couldn't do without them

              had to carry

                    to use them

Enslaved and stuck-up

              —how funny—

Eyes growing

          wider

            harder to bear

Inside me

        a churning

          a sickening

Forth and back   my black black hair   I found it so

I cut my black black hair

now what

Not a thing

—try it, please—

I'm day

      light

         loony

            breeze-borne

Good morning   wind swaying the apricot tree

Good morning   reborn one   set free

Now I wonder   at a pin's round head

That some weigh out   as a lifetime

Forth and back   from my black black hair   I cut myself free.

Translated by Saliha Paker and Mel Kenne

WINDOWS OF LONELINESS

We are out of our routine
Back of our eyes there is darkness
Upon separation we collapse
Our ties are broken
This is Istanbul.

There are some who, to our surprise,
Do not lose the warmth of their grasp,
The order of their lives, on separation.
We are amazed. This is Istanbul.

We move the night birds of Istanbul from one roof
And settle them on another.
These windows are windows of loneliness.
From outside, from above, with our eyes
We make it rain upon these windows

Translated by Özcan Yalım, William A. Fielder and Dionis C. Riggs

LAUGHING STOCK

A thousand times they made the man the laughing stock
They brought up fresh mirrors from below the ground
And held them up to the sun inside him
A thousand times they made the sun the laughing stock

So we could not truly gaze at the sun
Tiny and orange and pale
We knew that man to be God incalculable
Which means so chubby and stubby and pale

Translated by Talat S. Halman

MOUNTAIN AIR

Someone should rip this eastern air
Off the evening and carry it to daybreak
So daylight will burst on majestic mountains
And the white dove will stretch
That's just what I said

That's just what I said this black man
Defeated and routed and weary
Should turn my steps away from the familiar street
This man to whom I say nothing more than hello
This man I detest single-track and flat
He should carry them elsewhere
I dragged my solitude like my eyes
There should be no forgetting so I did not
I a quaint sad gypsy — that serves me right —
Before the peacock's bright feathers
Aware of its ugly legs
I forcibly fixed myself and never forgot
My hands were ugly and I had no grace
It was a lie and had I believed it
I should have died eternally
That's just what I said this black man
Takes a hold of my coat in cold drinks
Takes a hold of my scarf and my boredom
He knows not my loneliness I'm not scared
He can't clutch I can't love him nor do I fear
Oh you quaint sad gypsy

A black man should take this mountain air
And carry it to majestic mountains
So day may break and the white dove grow
And a quaint sad gypsy in the waters
Should shed his defeat and decay
So daylight may burst forth

Translated by Talat S. Halman

from *In the Shallows* (1964)

NOT THE FEAR OF SHIVERING

We are the tired warriors worn down by defeat after defeat
Too timid or ashamed to enjoy a drink
Someone gathers all the suns, keeps people waiting for them
It's not the fear of shivering but warming up
We are the tired warriors, so many loves frightened us off

They have held the mountain roads
The arrows are shot, the traps are set
Someone forgives our ugliness
In the name of friendship
We set out on flat roads again without arrows or rabbits
We are the daunted warriors, so many loves frightened us off

Translated by Talat S. Halman

WHO WHAT

All the doors held, long intervals
drawn gently into darkness, caressed
A belief, an earring, a colored glass
Let who will save what be guessed,
Yes, but not known

Much noise from small things
You're drawn into the world's din
A lapse, a full glance, a friendship
Then suddenly right at your side that fugitive

Let who will save what be guessed
Yes, but not known

A crowd of cats at the flimsy door
Scratch, beat, claw
Let death come with soft hands, soft fur
That door's not to be opened, no

Let who will save what be guessed
Yes, but not known

This is where the needle's happy at work
Three lovely little cats over there
Let them freeze silent
The crazy girl will keep to herself

Let who will save what be guessed
Yes, but not known

Translated by Saliha Paker and Mel Kenne

from *The Red Carnation* (1971)

AUTUMN

It is autumn, my eyes are blurred, I am blind
It is autumn, because my hair is falling
They say I was born on the high plains beyond the sea
Down, then uphill. The pain in my knees will ease

A song comes down the stream, beloved one
The fight is over, hang your gun on the wall
The hearth is king now, go to the forest
Take your axe from the corner, kiss the children

They are flying kites down below, the weather is right
The children down there can read, I am blind
Lovely the smell of books, of newspapers
If I could go down and smell the children too
I am bound to this place, beloved
I am blind and old, thirty years of age
Take the children with you and go down there
It is my wish. Take them and let them see

It is autumn, you are scantily clad, my darling
Myself, never mind. I have never crossed the brook
But I know the potatoes of one summer's toil
Will not provide a piece of serge for you
Ask, are we listed as living in their records
I am blind, we are old, see that the children are listed
Take the potatoes to market for twenty-five
Ride the donkey. Sing as you return.

Worldly goods are bought with the world's money
You have scratched twenty-five lira out of the earth
Buy a shroud. Buy the soap and sponge for it
Set aside the money the Hoja's money for Paradise

I shall die this autumn. My tasks are finished now
I have washed in the brook, climbed the walnut-tree, frightened birds
Been kidnapped. Borne twelve children. Cradled, watched
Married a son, lost a daughter, lived to be thirty
Do not weep, girl. And do not mind, my darling
I do not weep. Let the stones and mountains weep
I am blind. I am uncouth. I am overripe. I am sick
Where should I find those who have caused these things?
Let the birds weep, they grieve better than man

Translated by Nermin Menemencioğlu

WINTER

Winter is here. We have lighted a fire, beloved
The walnut has shed its leaves, the stream is cloudy
Death on his black horse has been warded off
There are beets boiling in the pot

Blow. We are smeared with smoke, we are dirty, bad
Blow. The more hell it is, the more familiar
Blow. Is God like a knife or like a hatchet
Blow with your blind woman's mouth, your only weapon

We wept, my daughter-in-law and I, yesterday
They shot my Mehmet Ali in the forest
Do not wear your best, I told him, there will be blood
They shot my Mehmet Ali in the forest

Hush. The more we are broken the better it is
Hush—Paradise. Hush—the blow of the mallet. Bring
The sacred book. We had already received
The evil omen from our frozen larder

My Mehmet Ali's head looked well on your pillow
We buried him—death from "natural" causes, they said
His clothes now fit my Osman well
The blood money went to the corporal

Is the sparrow a bird, the sprat a fish, are we human?
Do not weep, would you flood our graves with tears?
The dead must rest. Let Mehmed Ali go
We'll buy you flannel on market-day, and shiny shoes

It is morning now, but where is my daughter-in-law?
Kidnapped, and I must go to beg for her
Give her back, my master, my Selim Bey
We have nothing with which to buy another bride

Translated by Nermin Menemencioğlu

17

SPRING

Oh, no one's got the time
To stop'n think about fine things

With broad brush-strokes they move along
Sketching homes kids graves onto the world
Some are obviously lost when a rhyme starts up
With one look they shut it all out
And the rhyme enters the night, as fine things do

Some pus in your breasts, some fish, some tears
Sea sea sea you turn into a giant
Evenings your fog creeps up the river-mouths
Raids our hazel-nuts
What to do with their blackening buds
We beg our children: go hungry for a while
We beg the tycoons
Please, one less "Hotel," one secret marriage less to sketch
Please one less bank, a plea
From us to you and from you to those abroad

We send our wives out to get a manicure, to say
—sir, if you please—
We send our children out to beg
We're off on our way, our beds entrusted to God
Motorized gypsies of the summer

Oh, no one's got the time
To stop'n think about fine things

To return to the stream where we first bathed, our fathers' homes
Passion for the earth, for what it's being here
We plug our ears: money money money
We pull out the plugs: fight fight squabble
Someone may inquire: quarrel but why
An ever-grinding axe for our neighbor, a fist for our wife
Why the quarrel—we have no idea.

18

Then in our small town, that prison
We place our eraser before our eyes
With a shove we widen our days
We make room to give thought to our wives
To think about the bloom of the violet passing without us

Even if no one's got the time
To stop'n think about fine things
Even if the little schoolteachers
Multiply their holidays
And in the name of whatever we hold sacred
Weave blindfolds for our eyes
What's stored up and sketched will in time
Break into blossom as spring flowers

From across the stream over yonder
Some will whistle, we'll sound it back.

Translated by Saliha Paker and Mel Kenne

SUMMER

It's back the summer I love
With ants and flies we've crept along the earth
With red mullets, bluefish, leafy lettuce and olives
Way past fog-ridden April, depressing rains
Blue on the Black Sea, for kids to rejoice
For poets to rejoice, it's back the summer I love

We're in nineteen sixty-eight. We've seen the Forties and Fifties
We lived through the Sixties, with political statements
Committed crimes. May fifth at five p.m. in Kızılay
And all of us come from work elsewhere
To Ankara, the revolution's base

In the Forties we were seven. A draftee's hitch three years
They bragged about keeping us out of the War, they still do
When you're seven the rule is to go to school hungry
Beside wheat that rots, beside furs and diamonds
To go to school hungry. Maybe only a *simit*, an orange for lunch

To be skinny, ugly, ashamed of footwear
—having their long-lasting effects—
Tooth disease, disease of the hair
Trembling hands, sudden heart tremors
Scared of being shamed, ashamed
No candy, no ball, no dolls
For days weeping, notebook, pencil, book,
—the lasting effects when loneliness strikes—
They bragged the War's far away from us
—The War's far from us, thanks to our cleverness
Then let's have just one more villa, one more fur coat, one more trip to
          Europe
Well-nourished, white as white peals of laughter in black automobiles
Sometimes a bunch of parsley, a basket of eggs
In return for a salary of fifty *lira* and ninety *kuruş* a soldier's ration
Black black black
Ankara

20

War outside, as a New Rome is built
An Old Rome demolished
A world where wolves lounge about with songs on their lips
Dogs in a long spring heat
Blood, fire, endless starving, rotting Europe
With its trusts, banks and stock exchanges
At their keenest in virtue and bravery and treachery

Year nineteen fifty. It was back the summer I love
I believe we weren't even seventeen yet, in our old age
Not even seventeen, I believe, still back in our childhood
Who stirred up everything, with what right, for what
How had we multiplied so quickly
In love, in shame, in indifference, in grudge
In forgiveness, in forgiveness that ruins that clouds

The months of May are beautiful, with their brave
Stoneworkers who pierce holes to let the stream flow
With folk singers, swearing fishermen
Gravediggers, girls gathering snails,
Chatty, smiling women, wool spinners
Those struck by epidemics, sharp market sellers
But above all with their revolutionaries, oh those revolutionaries
Who, mistake after mistake become ever more unmistaken
The May months are beautiful.

For the sake of cancer ladies and gentleman dance all night long
In return for receipts, pity is bestowed on the blind and the poor
In black headlines, "An incomparable, invaluable person"
For businessmen with no work to be done.

Summer I love is here for clothes in mothballs
For moldy pickles, rotting jams
For stinking awareness-raisers glued to their chairs
—Oh the remedy you claim to be that's not true remedy.
Summer I love is here with its minstrels and bards

Troubled ones, pencil-browed ones, lousy-haired ones
Nylon-stockinged women, scabby-horsed men
Summer is back to Anatolia
To Anatolia
Oh the remedy you claim to be that's not true remedy.
You sit where you are, don't move
Like a socialist Jesus once in a while drop by
Stand aside, so you can take the center when the time's ripe
May comes down to Anatolia from its own springs
May comes down to Anatolia from its own mountains
The summer I love it's back

Translated by Saliha Paker and Mel Kenne

Anatolian Ellas and the Statues

More heavy-hearted the more she speaks,
More guilty as she does so. As if fed
Again and again on impossible things, nauseous
Strains from her voice thread out to the world
Facing one two three statues of mud
Upright, she shouts. Each move she makes
Each move of hers, crumbling.

Yet
Always there were warm rooms somewhere
In warm rooms, ancient men
Quiet men, their forefathers
Who performed miracles, holy men, saints
At their headstones also candles were lit
Birds also flew about their shoulder-points
White birds
Then with birds they all came to this run-down room.
For two hundred years they walked
They boarded Captain Dursun's ship
Hoisted their sails in the Black Sea's midst
Storm. Passengers offered prayers
A white-bearded man
Hail captain. Who could that be who who
As quickly as he'd appeared, vanished.
The storm winds laid.
The sails were struck, the helm stayed steady.
Somebody told the story at Ünye
No sooner had it been reported
Than the birds vanished. The candles gone out
In closets ancestors died
The ordeal persisted. It will go on
In the hearth-homes.

Everyone will die, will one day die
God will remain. The hearth will burn.

Some will always remain in that room.
They will smile, bow their heads, sigh.
They will keep wickedness a secret
Speak out the good
In long, white robes, soft and delicate.
A shapeless stone on the table, her hand
To hide, but why. One of the statues laughs
—They've trod you down.
—Is that me or you? Look closely.
Breathing in from the people, breathing onto them
Oh filthy mud of the city, is that me or you?
Now her hand at rest on the table
Has taken on some character
Slowly she will raise it
The table will shake. In the end
It will most surely topple over
The hand will grow soft, become refined
A bunch of bright yellow daffodils
On the green corn a slight breeze
On the earth, festivity, *alahey*
Machines, girls hand in hand.

—Some manners from Paris, a statue says
Let's educate the cities. The villages... Oh, they're so coarse
—Only you, dear God, would know,
My forefather, my saint, where are you
You, who with birds above your shoulders
Rallied the scattering soldiers together
Guided the ships to safety
Rattled the statues as they fled to their ease

The end of the tangled yarn will be found
On the embers potatoes will bake, coffee pots simmer
On the path in front of the window
The sick are carried off on planks, as are the dead
Anger is not broken shoulders, lifeless legs
Anger is the corpse fallen from the plank

Anger, the mystery in books, cracks open, released
The end of the tangled yarn is found

Breaths drawn from the people
Whispered back to them as awareness
Living like, living with, the people

Translated by Saliha Paker and Mel Kenne

THREE MASTERS TO ONE CAPTIVE

I spent the summer in tremors, dear master
Reading omens, divining dreams, conversing with water
I don't see, but I can tell. A heavy weight on my chest
Perhaps it's a tiny woman not I
A bait for the falcon chained to your arm
A frightened sparrow for its mouth

The bird flew off, you mounted a pure Arabian stallion,
Your horseblock a live shoulder,
Riding pillion, three ivory girls and a dark boy
"Mama" they'd call out to me
Their faces wore your image and mine
Therefore, with hardly a doubt,
You were my husband, my precious master.

I can't remember but it was said
One day you came home listless
"Sweet are the street fountains, bitter is home
Sweet are the streets, bitter is home
Sweet is the meal spread by others, bitter is home"
—Oh just let me die, master—
You picked me up hurled me to the ground
I was not a little girl, perhaps some stone
For fathers love their little girls
As I've seen in others

You were the city's dark outlaw, beloved master
Off to the mountains your falcon on your arm
You rode your horse, held your whip
Your voice, churchbells heralding a holy day
A clear bugle call for the barracks, shepherds' whistle to the water
I loved you so much, oh so much
Then one day, with bared teeth, a dark look in your eyes
—Oh just let me die, master—

"This is no joke," you said. "As your son,
 I am your supreme master from now on."

Translated by Saliha Paker and Mel Kenne

Rust

I went to my native city to clean off some rust,
To visit some stones on site, excavations etc.
As a sign of respect I tied my long hair back
And put on country clogs
So I wouldn't be lost in the earth and dust.

They stood on the edge of the town to meet me,
Surrounding and cutting me off.
I never thought I would be a guest to my childhood.
I never imagined the very first step of rejection
Would come from meeting with my women-folk.

I never imagined children sent out to school
To streets and parks,
Or inns and hotels built on my beloved ruins,
Cakes instead of saffron pilaf in the windows.
I never dreamt of icecream made from ice instead of snow,
And not a single Çapanoğlu left in Yozgat.

Grandfather's dead, grandmother's dead, my mother's dead,
I couldn't visit our old home.
Grandfather who for years survived
The ravages of grief and tobacco,
Grandmother who for years survived
Ravaged by poverty and grandfather's ruin,
Mother who for years survived
An incurable wasting away.

From now on I'm not Gülten from Yozgat,
Wherever I die I belong.
Let me die in the eastern regions
By the cold waters of the trackless mountains.

Translated by Ruth Christie

WOMAN'S SONG

It's time to leave, the day of banishment's upon us,
Exile is here again,
I've packed the books and dressed the kids,
Let's make for the snows of Dranaz.

Wherever we go, the people are poor as mice.
Every spring and summer far from home
We return to our native place but know
Neither our place of exile nor our roots.
We picked a crocus in the Ardahan uplands,
A narcissus at Sinop,
The yellow rose at Van,
The orange fragrance came from Kumluca.
We confused home and exile,
Exiles like us were never known before.

It's time to leave, the day of banishment's upon us,
In your absence the shoots you set will grow,
Shake in the wind and shelter from the sun.
It's nature's law the crops will ripen,
The infant find its tongue and fragile form,
The mist will vanish from Isfendiyar's top.

Greetings from us to those who've gone before,
Greetings to friends and kin, to those who suffer,
Greetings to those who endure,
My pity is for the helpless, don't look at my tears.

It's time to leave, the day of banishment is here.
Don't ask where is our country and our native land.

Translated by Ruth Christie

from *Laments and Songs* (1976)

A VOICED LAMENT

Who's sprinkled salt on our children's milk
Who's muddied our waters
Hey, who goes there?

Are we living a fairy-tale, which century is this
Whence can the poison have seeped
Into our apple, onto our comb?

The light of day comes to our room unbidden
Wakes us and takes us away, forces
A pick-axe, a pen into our hands
The wagonloads go past, go past
Pushed into harness, we climb the slope

We pluck night from the forty thieves
Sing it a lullaby in our arms
Should not its arms enfold our sleep
Who is rocking whom?

They are walking the dead away
.Mindful of proper ceremony
Is that the wind, is someone blowing
The living are in their lockers
Then who is it whose breath
Ruffles these well-kept files
Hey, who goes there?

Translated by Nermin Menemencioğlu

LAMENT OF THE WORKING MOTHER'S CHILD

I threw them out. What good are paints
For loneliness, apart from black
What color can I use
Dry table, dull ceiling, sulky carpet
My pictures should look pale

My window no longer attracts birds
Daffodils are losing their breath
Even with three brushes, you still can't comb Yuku-Lili's hair
I am the child of a mother who goes out to work

Snow on the road and the roof veils
The blue lines left over from last summer
I say nothing. Trying once or twice
The sound of joy will also say nothing
Cat-like wails at the foot of the wall
In the gardens, ugly chrysanthemums should be blooming

Translated by Cemal Demircioğlu, Arzu Eker, Sidney Wade and Mel Kenne

SONG OF A DWELLER IN A HIGH-RISE BLOCK

They piled the houses high,
in front long balconies.
Far below was water
far below were trees

They piled the houses high,
a thousand stairs to climb.
The outlook a far cry
and friendships further still.

They piled the houses high
in glass and concrete drowned.
In our wisdom we forgot
the earth that was remote
and those who stayed earthbound.

Translated by Ruth Christie

SONG TO AN AGELESS WOMAN

Your face was never a rough sketch
its lines were a finished drawing.
You drew on your own face
in the midst of loves and fears and longings.
You wove satin cut woollen cloth,
you were tailor and dressmaker.
Bodies of the people fat and thin were clad
in your school pinafores and prison garb.

You weighed up praises from your daily life
against the losses of a higher one
and cursed the difference.
Perhaps now you're outside your body
in a silence
where everything even the smallest atom
arises and moves together.
From within silence a little late maybe
your woman's mother's maker's hand
will gather their needs again.
We brought you roseleaves from the mountains
and made you a pillow.
Now rest your white head.

Translated by Ruth Christie

ANGRY LAMENT

Beat your innocent children,
get them used to punishment young;
in a world where there's more punishment than crime
beat your children.

If their eyes are wider than the skies,
get them used to blinkers, like horses;
if they learn to give instead of take
slap their hands hard.

Is anything more precious than life?
Your native land?
Can friendship be eaten or drunk?
And love—what use is love?

Translated by Ruth Christie

from *Hymns* (1983)

HYMN OF THE DESPAIRING POET

I'm tinier than a birdseed
Although the world can fit inside me
I can't fit into the worlds
I can't fit in, my son

If only I could be a cloud, I would
If only I could rise up to the sky, I would
I'd drift over the autumn meadows
But I can't rain, my son

My hawk is fettered
With a carnation in its beak
It's this tremendous contradiction
I can't unravel, my son

A poet, I came stumbling on a dream
then I turned and came to the struggle
I've hung up my frenzied pencil
I can't write a word, my son

Translated by Saliha Paker and Mel Kenne

Hymn for Patience

Invited, I came lingered long
stopped as if for good while people laughed on
as if about to leave I smile

A fret-saw in my heart
round and round I pace on a burning stone
I'm the unloving ant of life
If racing the day I touch my body
Does it hurt, as it did once, where they hit me
I may have come to feel at home

No word from whom I long for, the silenced one
Nothing, I'm burnt from love
I'm silvered niello, I'll never wear down
Trying patience now

Translated by Saliha Paker and Mel Kenne

HYMN FOR THE BELIEVER

On our lifetime's kilim
Words stitched in our mother's tongue
Go this way, mostly:
Hold pain and suffering at bay
With a silk fan in your hand
Gently, quietly, with tolerance
Come up to yourself
There, that's you, there, that mirror of calm waters
Watch, smile

Yet
Who doesn't fan her heart's fire to a blaze
Doesn't let her doomsday grow
And doesn't hold herself strictly to account
Won't save herself from the flames

Whoever's truly upright
Should search for Joseph in the well in Canaan
Not in Egypt when he's sultan
Oh believer
You, oh believer
Speak to yourself without using a broker

Translated by Saliha Paker and Mel Kenne

37

HYMN FOR THE ROSE

People grew accustomed
To exchanging a rose for a title-deed
To changing other people's lives
Is life a wicker chair
They grew accustomed to arranging then removing
Heart and honor, they grew accustomed
Is honor a leaf to be blown away by the breeze
The heart trampled upon like weeds
No one thinks at all of the other
Nor cares to know himself
If it's not human to know thyself
How can the human be

This is why the world, oh, the great big world,
Turns into a land of the dead
Those who for now keep silent
Those who've fallen outside the game
Only they will rise to their feet
When the day comes to doom

Translated by Saliha Paker and Mel Kenne

Poems of 42 Days (1986)

1.

The tyrant's night is one with the night of the wronged one
And a longer night awaits the one whose verdict is tyranny
Agony's cry, screams, imprecations
Can pass through the needle's eye
Feel their way through the killer, the executioner
To arrive finally at the doorway, the reason, the why.

2.

THE AFTERMATH

Tall, purple flowers bloomed in the little park at the centre of the square. A bed full of purple flowers. Could this be a coincidence? That doesn't seem possible. If you asked the gardener who had kept them in seed, he'd say, "They were meant to be red, yellow, and white. I don't know how they all turned out to be purple."

He should know—if he's seen us there, watched us on winter days. As he's been put in charge of that impressive district, he should be a good gardener. If he's a good gardener, then he should know why his flowers had taken on that alien color.

Purple. Seeps in from sorrow. From human agony. Drains into earth with our bodies' electricity. What else to expect but purple flowers?

We were mothers. We returned from visits, from the prison where our sons and daughters were kept. Before, we used to scatter away, but during these days of hunger it never crossed our minds to do that. We stayed together. Walked all the length of the streets. Crammed into buses. On our way to reach the authorities in stately buildings. We sought relief in petitions, in more petitions and countless stamps.

It was cold. Most of us wore flimsy clothes, old, thin-soled shoes which soaked up the wet. We were here every day, sitting in that little round park.

They chased us from the doors. Scolded and pushed us away. Some-times we fought them back. Shouted in anger. But we couldn't put up with that for long, we couldn't hold on. We went back to the little round park. Parks are for the public. Who could be angry with us, sitting there quietly? Did we sit there quietly? Yes. The most we could do was whisper to one other. What can we do, what should we do? But storms raged in our bod-ies. Our silence filled the world with siren-shrieks and screams. What does it matter if it's five or ten people shouting? The ones that really matter are the quiet ones. Ask the silent one what after-shocks rock her body, what cataclysms it releases into air and earth. We used to watch how people be-haved towards us. There'd be respectful silence on the streets and on the bus. Those on duty would suddenly appear confused and listless, ready to get up and quit work any moment.

The earth—the earth we trod on, the earth that blessed us with the mud, the puddles, the wet and the cold—received our pain, our anger.

We sat in that park for days. We stood and waited. On the earth where the purple flowers bloomed. If the gardener happened to see us, he could explain why the blossoms were purple instead of yellow, red and white, and why they stood so upright and tall.

3.

THE YARD

A scream completed the yard
Without it a part would've been missing
Congealing into long icicles
The scream froze solid

The scream froze solid
Drawing deep blue pictures over us
Where d' you get that scream from mother
Thought the guard, from the sirens,
Perhaps from the seagulls
But where's the sea? There has to be one
Since above there's the cold, blue-curdled sky
And below,

Underneath, beside, all through us
The yard.

The yard within which one day in seven
We were drawn together and scattered apart
And that became a living part of us.

The yard
With its huts and wiry barbs
And a guard's pink scowl
On those other six days how could
The slate-colored roof have ever held
The silence preceding
An earthquake

It could never be whole without that scream
With its rifles pointed at us
Its noisy mechanical sounds
The scream came to make it so
It was a black-bodied wreath drifting about the yard
Its woven flowers of curse
Growing
So big
As it paused before each mother
It could only be deemed a mountain
So now
How do we mothers
Still fit in that yard?

4.

THE YARD

The scream stretched out longer and longer. Circled the yard. Wrapped up
the rooftops and chimneys. Made its sure way through stone or iron.
Reached into the sky. Chased off the cranes. Faded the blue. Touched the
scrawny force-fed trees and uninviting flowers, dove into the distant pool

and bounced out again. Hit the sentinels' huts. Rattled the stacked rifles. His strings jerked suddenly, the sergeant sprang into action, called his men to attention, gave them orders. Rifles in hand they marched forward. In the inner yard stood the woman. The scream continued.

Holding her by the arms, they half walked, half dragged her away. The scream turned to imprecations. Sustained its pitch."You ...gots, you've killed my son, You a.. ....kers, now kill me too."

The scream had gathered momentum. It carried on even as the woman became quiet.

They took her into an annex with a low roof, where she collapsed on the ground. They eyed each other while holding her arms. Should they pick her up or let her lie there? Should they stand her on her feet or allow her to sit? This was an unknown situation, something befalling the officials for the first time. This silent crowd, they who could only weep and let their tears trickle into their hearts, had been commanded officially for years. Official advice, official shouts, and the official reprimands flung at them was all they got. Occasional rough play was only one order of business among others.

The incredible had happened. From that quiet, helpless, skinny woman a scream had leapt and left her utterly empty. She marvelled at how she'd freed the scream that had been keeping her alive and on her feet. Should she remain lying as she was, get up, or sit down?

"What are you screaming about, woman?" the man in charge would have asked had he been there on time and been standing beside her. By the time he came running in, the woman was already curled up in a ball on the floor.

His anger faded. For a moment he considered helping her up and giving her a seat. Just as his voice was about to escape from his throat and say "She's just a mother," the official in him crushed it.

"Hurry up and write a report, this woman has insulted us!"
"Yes, sir."

Who knows what place the woman—crossing mountains, ridges, and waterways—had set out from to see her son. For five minutes. Only that long. "How're you, all right?" "I'm all right, and you?" "I'm all right." "How're father and sister?" "All well." "D'you want me to get you anything?"

Only a foolish writer would add more words here. It's clear to everyone her time would be up by now. Up without casting a last glance, up without catching a smile or final gesture.

42

No matter. The mother comes anyway. A three-day journey. Across mountains and rivers. Piling with others out of puffing trains or buses at stations. Piling into crammed vehicles like just another bundle. Appearing at the doorway that leads to her son.

Although visitations had been banned, for some reason a few were still allowed. Rumour had it that many a building in the towns and villages had been burnt to ashes by those being held. They were chained, beaten, attacked by dogs. Kicked. Their testicles stomped on, crushed. The mother had heard bits of this while she waited for her name to be called out. She waited but her son's name wasn't among those banned from visitation. She felt a secret joy, then shame. She looked around at the women with faces blurred by agony. She again felt ashamed, her joy evaporated. She felt uneasy being one of the privileged who were admitted. She felt upset with her son. "Why had he been set apart? How will these mothers look at me now?"

"Just let me see him," she said to herself, "just let me go in and see him."

She entered and saw that her son could hardly stand. His head was bandaged, he could barely be understood.

"See, mother, this is how I am, now go away, I can't stand up any longer."

She got it at once. The onus of being set apart was not on the shoulders of her son. It was they, they, they, who had set some apart to display them. Maybe to intimidate, maybe for some other reason.

For awhile she looked about in confusion and then walked out and down the stairs. Once outside, she saw the other mothers. The stacked rifles. The dogs. It was then that the scream forced its way out of her heart, her lungs, her throat. Exploded from her mouth. Not stopping, ever. It wasn't she who was screaming but the scream itself.

The mothers in the prison yard weren't prepared yet to gather up the scream and find a place for it. Moving about them, the scream went berserk, slipped into bags of clean laundry, brushed headscarves and hair, both hennaed and gray, and chafed against poorly shod feet.

"Oh, who knows how her son is?" thought the mothers. "And what about the girls, are they also...?

Those banned from visitation looked all done in. A knife couldn't pry any words out of them. How were *their* children doing? Two mothers fainted right off. They were picked up and stretched out on the benches. Most of the others were quietly weeping.

The scream invaded their tears and dried them up. Awakened those who had fainted. Snagged collars and shook people up. Broke in on the officials. Howled out the barking dogs.

Silence.

For its own sake the report was written. And, for the sake of it, signed.

"Can you sign?" they asked the mother.

"Yes," she said.

"Then sign here."

She did. She was once more herself. "My son's had it, he's all burnt out. Go ahead, kill me too, what do I care anymore."

"Take her upstairs, boy."

She was escorted upstairs. As she mounted the steps, herself again, she thought of what she would say. She expected some cannonball to be fired at her thunderously. Reprimands and humiliation.

As she opened the door, went in, and stood surrounded by men with rifles, someone shouted out her name while waving the report.

"Why did you scream like that? Why did you swear, why did you have to speak such words?"

"I saw my son in there, in that state,... you've crushed my baby to bits, what else could I do? What more do I have to fear? What's left but my life, take that too, for my salvation.

Looking thoughtful and upset, not likely now to submit to the official in him, the official laid the report on his desk.

"Bring her son, let them sit down face to face. Let her see her son's not dead, let her see these people have seven lives. Nothing ever really happens to them."

"May the wind drive those words away from your mouth."

They brought in her son and offered them chairs. Holding the hands of her son, she kissed and caressed his face.

"So," thought the mother, "it was best to let that scream go, and not hold it down." She smiled.

The scream had done its job. For now. Quietly it flew off and claimed a corner near the far end of the eave. Where it hung on.

It can be seen by anyone who looks there.

5.

AT THE TABLE

It wasn't I but my death who sat at the table
The cheese gobbled me up, and so did the olive
While reaching for the bread, my hands dropped
My eyes burnt by the apple, I was left blind
A flood that wasn't mere water swept me away
It wasn't I but my death who sat at the table

6.

TABLE SETTING

So much to eat up, so much there to be eaten, to eat.

"What makes us any different from pigs and cows?" she thought, "just like them, we never stop chewing the cud."

In her childhood and youth, accounts could be kept of what was shopped for, of what was cooked or let go to waste. Now, there are thousands of kinds of everything.

She picked up the pot from the stove, brought it directly over and set it down on the table. Was it the tightness in her chest, or nausea? Not knowing which, she shouted,

"Like cattle, you're just like cattle! Never quit eating, do you? One meal no more over than it's time for the next one! Why do you have to eat so much, why?"

At the table six heads raised up. Turned their faces towards the mother. Instantly alert to the memory. Then lowered again. Bending even lower till they were no longer there. Snails, tortoises, all curled up, they slipped quietly beneath the table.

The daily ritual, the poisonous, fatal ritual was in progress. It's taken over mealtime thanksgiving in some households now.

Like a bird of prey, the mother vented her anger on the father:

"While my brave boy, always hungry, is growing ash-pale in there, turning into a corpse, you gorge yourself like a pig, a pig, a pig! Just look at

45

that face of yours, that body! You never want for food and drink. All your needs met. Each and every craving of your body…"

Ashamed, very much ashamed, the father quietly arose and, not knowing how deep the mother would go in her anger and what she would bring up, let loose an urgent shout:

"Shut up, woman, close your mouth! What is it you want from me at every meal? What power do I have to do anything? These kids are ours too, is there no pity to be spared for them? Are you blind, can't you see how hard each mouthful goes down our throats. Afterwards you regret it and plead with us, "Come on, sit down and eat." This is life. It goes on. What more can be done?"

The ritual had picked up enough speed. It was bound to die down. Inexorably.

The mother was a fine cook. She turned down her voice's fire. Folded back her pain, making it easier to swallow.

"I can't stand it! Don't be upset with me, don't be hurt. I just can't bear it. They're in there, just like that. Knowing everything."

Her voice died away. Six famished, anxious mouths bent hurriedly over their plates. Six noses furtively drew in the aroma of the meal. Hands had no choice but to reach out for the spoons. The mother folded in her righteousness. Set it out where it could be seen. Casually. As if she might choose to unfold it. Then she rolled out her regret.

"Come on," she said. "Hurry, it's getting cold."

7.

Your Face, While Laughing

Your face, while laughing
The cooing of a dove
The unheeded growth of grass
Fairgrounds and spring festivals
All else besides the habitual

Your face, while laughing
Overcomes the pains of the past,
Transforms itself into tomorrow

So it seems that, while laughing
You've smashed your cross
Yours and the one borne by others who'll follow
Her halo having slipped over her brow
The night sits weeping to herself

So deeply do I long for this in my soul,
With such passion in my heart,
In my mind you must always remain so.

8.

LAUGHING

What happens when the hopeless wound of a devastating love is bound to
long years of suffering and the pains of captivity?

He's a delicate lad, full of feeling — one who echoes back a single touch
a thousand times.

The boy has turned in on himself and lived there for nearly a year now.
On the verge of leaving at any moment. Ready to kill himself. Or observing
his march inward, never to return. Like one become lost in a black passion.

How will the mother — who may only see him for five minutes once a
week to say nothing more than "How are you?" — reach out to him, get him
to abandon his paths of no return?

She falls to pieces. Can't stop herself from crying, "I've got to do some-
thing. Something's just got to be done." Helplessness as well creeps up on
her. "We need some kind of miracle to bring the boy back, " she mutters
and moans lying sleepless all night.

Then one day hunger strikes. Finding out, the mother said, "That's it.
The end. It's over. Our hands fall to our sides."

On her next visit, as she stood before him on the other side of the wire,
she searched for the boy's face. There it was. Searched his eyes. There they
were. Searched for some expression. Everything frozen. She could find
none there.

So when will she ever see him laughing again — the laugh that seemed
to leap away from his beautiful teeth, irrepressible, darting about his lovely

nose and lips, his eyes and cheeks, before bounding off? Or will she never again see it?

On the second visit the mother made during the hunger, the boy had a surprise for her. He must have cut his inner journey short, right there. "Gotta' go back," he must have said. Made up his mind to break free of his retreat. He still didn't smile, or laugh, but looked determined, wholly and purposefully one with himself, like a cannon ball.

In an instant, the mother was hopeful. The middle of her chest showed an out-of-season vine shoot. For the moment she kept it hidden, just in case. Let it be seen by no one.

In the third week of hunger, the boy had trouble speaking, but his mind was ticking along like a clock. His heart was warm.

Up until then, even if she'd wept tears of blood, the mother never would've thought of saying, "You're going to die, boy, and you shouldn't. Quit the hunger."

Without a word she left.

In week four, after six anxious days, she couldn't bear looking upon a body of skin and bones. "Give it up, son," her eyes begged. No word left her mouth.

She expected no response. She got none.

For many visits, like some newly invented form of torture, this went on. On the forty-third day, the fast broken, the boy could no longer stand. Like a branch, he swayed, only able by twisting his tongue to utter a few words.

The mother let loose all the breath left in her chest, "Don't die, son, don't! You won't, will you?

The sparkle now gone from his eyes, the boy let out a laugh, skin clinging tight to his cheeks, through lips barely open but with teeth gleaming white, so full of life, so lovely a laugh!

Picking him up, the mother nestled him beneath her largest wing feather, then like a ball of light shot away.

Even yet she flies.

9.

My Left Alone Won't Do

Your cuffs bind my arms too
My right hand won't hold, can't clutch
My magic's left me, my poetry's gone
My left alone won't do

10.

Released

Three long years later he was set free—three grievous, how dearly beloved years. His body had consumed itself, now there was nothing to be seen but a framework of bones. It was the twenty-fifth day of hunger. Those of his mates who seemed stronger bundled up his clothes. Half stooping half dragging himself, one arm numb and useless, eyes empty of light, he was taken away—and left to wait outside. While helping him leave, they had supported his arms. He could never have said, "Let go of me, you caused this, I don't need you."

His throat was sore, his tongue bound up. Not a single word, nary a sound. For an eternity he waited out there, just where they'd left him. Then his father and big brother came to take him away. They lifted him in their arms and settled him into the car.

Slowly, very slowly, he got back to feeding himself. After a few days he was up on his feet. He could walk. Estranged to everything and everybody. He couldn't have imagined how in three years things at home could change so much. And he felt tense and troubled under the weight of the secret guilt of having been freed and leaving his friends behind.

All eyes at home were fixed on his. Anything he asked for was there in his hands in an instant, and whatever he felt like eating—right there in his mouth. It horrified him to see the prisonhouse his own home had become. "Stay in, don't go out yet, take your time, pull yourself together first, what if you're followed!" His mother wept:

"I won't be able to stand it if they take you away from me again,!"

His betrothed, his father, his big brother.

He had to survive the loneliness that deeply and stealthily dug into his bones. Verging on tears when you touched him, he couldn't utter a word about happiness or speak of all the desires he yearned to satisfy.

It wasn't long until—slinging over his shoulder all the promises and vows, the concern overbrimming the eyes of his mother and his betrothed, the anger that was about to sprout again in his father—he was out on the streets.

He had heard of the mothers who were gathering in the parks, trailing off toward the doorways. So he went out there but kept his distance, never approaching them.

"They know what to do, what's right."

As they leave the court hearings like wounded birds with drooping wings, the mothers yell to one another: "Why are we waiting? For what? What more are we waiting for? Are we going to let them die? Let's go!"

From one end of the city to the other they flew, no remedy in sight. Soaking up the day's ordeals and weariness. In groups they fluttered about and alighted in some public square, then away they went to stand at the doors.

There they were, right out in front of the country's supreme edifice. Intimidated by the splendour of the stonework. Creeping up towards the door. An official hustled forward to drive them off, working hard with his hands, arms and voice. Gradually the crowd gave in, backing away from the door. A few mothers tried to hold their ground, calling out to the others. Then, at last feeling overcome, they too bowed their heads and got ready to go.

At the bus stop was the man who had been released. Planning to board whatever bus for whatever destination.

The mothers were on the verge of scattering when the man lost his head. Lifting arms no thicker than rolling pins, he started to wave at them. The mothers saw him as they glanced around nervously. They didn't know who the man was, just somebody who'd catch a bus and take off to wherever. But no! Surely he was calling out to them! Gesticulating desperately. In fact he did get on a bus. He boarded the first one that came along. In the late afternoon light he stood beside the window staring out at the mothers with their eyes fixed on him and signalled them with his hands, arms and lips: "Stay where you are, sit there, don't go away. Don't leave!"

One mother called to the others: "Let's stay put, let's not leave!"

They stayed. Not only that, but they sat down on the roadsides. Until a better class of cars than any others in the city drove up to the supreme edifice and started to collect all the higher-ups of the city.

Throwing themselves in front of every car, the mothers shouted:

"Our sons and daughters are dying. What're you waiting for? Stop them from dying!"

Even as they were being grasped by iron hands, clutched by their coats or arms to be pulled or pushed away, they wouldn't retreat. Nor would they consider scattering.

Then, only then, did a clever official rush from the supreme door of the supreme edifice. In mellow tones, he summoned the mothers into the courtyard. Out of the public eye. With studied politeness some of the mothers were led inside. Ushered right into the edifice itself, where they were presented to a higher official. There they were permitted to give their account once more — "calmly."

When the man who had been released heard about this, he was filled with joy. He was so joyful, in fact, that he found enough inner strength to get rid of all his feelings of oppression and guilt. Flinging open the door of his house, of his room, he kicked them all out. Then, giving his mother a kiss, giving his betrothed a kiss, he shouted to his sister: "Hey, kid, you've really got big since the last time I saw you!"

11.

TOMORROW

Again and again, brother, I die
Then come back to life
Sister, don't give it a thought
Cast it aside
Tomorrow your head will ache too
Just as mine does tonight

12.

The Mother of One of the Others

Since she's always tired, she takes the bus from the first stop. To get to the prison, six long streets, as many shopping arcades and public squares have got to be passed. She was able to catch the bus just as it was leaving and was panting as she sat on the only empty seat she saw. Once she'd collected herself she was able to glance around. They were crossing the second square along the way, beside the Statue. The roads and shops were busy as beehives, people everywhere, charmed from their homes by the balmy spring weather. But the sky is gathering clouds. Rain is on its way. A pity.

As always, when the bus reached the second stop it was greeted by a chafing crowd. People pushed and shoved their way through as it took in its full load. The old bus was feeling the strain. Which "new" one would ever go as far out as those hills and slopes, drive through lanes hardly fit for two vehicles to pass together?

Those standing were finding it more than difficult, not knowing which bar to grab, or how to shrink back from the bodies pressing harder and harder from all sides.

Then she saw the woman. Standing back a bit, more troubled then the rest because of her age. Clutching the bar on the seat in front of her with one hand, a plastic bag in the other. The writing on the plastic said it clearly: mother of (…), in ward (…). In her own seat, the woman thought, "She's like me." Mother of a son. More than half the busload were like them, on the way to a visitation.

As she stood the mother was glancing around nervously, her eyes on the seated young people. If only one of them would get up, saying, "Come sit down, mother. " But none did. And staying on her feet was becoming unbearable for her.

The seated woman felt nervous too. She couldn't take her eyes off the older one.

Unable to wait longer, she signalled her.

"Come sit down, sister, I've rested a bit".

The other wasn't shy about accepting the offer.

"May God be pleased with you, I was about to collapse. Those young ones, they never say, You're elderly, take my seat. After all it's us who have to stand up for each other."

On her feet now, the woman didn't wait long to ask:

"Your boy, which case is he being tried in?

"No idea! How would I know which?"

She was somewhat irritated.

In a low voice the other pressed on:

"Right or left?"

The sitting woman didn't utter a word, pretended she didn't hear. The other one didn't give up:

"Is he with the ones in hunger? Given visitation rights?"

The answer came from another woman, sitting in the row behind with a child on her lap:

"I know this lady. The ones of ours only do their fasting during Ramazan, the holy month. What about yours? Is he in there with the fasting ones?"

The standing woman felt stunned. She hadn't expected this sudden attack. So—she'd given up her seat to a mother of one of the others! Her anguish at her son's hunger, that long-lasting hunger, now lay in shreds. "Have I done wrong?" she wondered, but then shame overcame her: "What does it matter, she's a mother too." All at once she felt like talking, like telling them all about it. No matter who it was, she had to let them know about her pain. Before her appeared all those she'd seen in hospital, in the prison sanatorium, at the hearings. So many of them there were, so many that she'd forgotten all about those people who went about their lives as if nothing was happening at the exact place where these others were locked in a life or death struggle!

"It's been thirty days now, sister. For thirty full days now they've been wasting away."

"So why the fasting? What's it about?"

"They just want to live like human beings. Without beatings, without wickedness. They've chosen to die, to die for their honor."

"Hush up, ask forgiveness...! To take their God-given life! Such twisted thoughts!"

The woman on her feet felt regret mixing in with her pain. The other sensed this.

"Listen now, don't mind what I say. You're a good mother. Your son has to be good too. I'll pray for him along with the others, just don't worry."

The regret between them melted away.

"I've heard your boys are feeding ours sweet water and such.

The older woman felt proud and pleased:

"Good, that's how it should be. A person should be there for his suffering fellows."

The standing woman felt warmed by this. She herself was perishing in dread of her son's dying. In her heart light dawned. "That's human," she thought.

"Human! Cherishing hope is only human!"

They stepped off the bus together. Queuing up before the barred door, one stood behind the other

13

FOG

The wolf comes running, let it come on
Slinking along, the wily fox comes
Let it come on
Our flock's held fast in its fold, but—
If there's no relief near enough
If we're one with the fog blocking the way
Let the fox or the wolf come on

14.

HONOR

She came twice a month at first, but with the start of hunger she made it every week. She'd take the evening train. Usually she'd sit up awake all night. In the morning, on her arrival in the city, she'd head straight for the prison where her daughter was kept. Following the visit she went back the way she'd come.

She hadn't seen her daughter for four weeks now. How she hoped and prayed this week they'd allow her a visit!

All this coming, going and waiting seemed utterly useless to her. It made her feel stupid. Coming such a long long way. With nothing in hand but a few pieces of clean underwear. All this waiting. Then going away again and leaving her. If she hadn't felt that doing all this meant something to her daughter, she'd have gone mad. These autumn days near winter were cooler. She shivered as she straightened the gray headscarf that came down to her eyebrows and tried to brace herself by snuggling down into her thin coat. She was reciting all her prayers. She never stopped reciting. She didn't like people to see her lips moving, but still she couldn't stop. She tried to drive away the thought of thirty days of hunger. It frightened her. She might lose her composure and cry, faint, or shout, doing things that didn't befit her age or her past. So she shooed hunger from her mind. Treated it as if it weren't there, didn't exist. It was good that they denied her a visit. The mothers who had seen their children looked wretched. So she recited her prayers. Never stopping. Praying was good for her. It set her mind at ease and strengthened her. When they read out her name, she took her place in the queue, bundle in hand. She was searched. Then she was directed to the courtyard with sharp, clipped commands. Added to those who had already been admitted, they made up a good-sized crowd. As if they were all stuck together in a ball, they heaved ahead to wait. And waited. She went on saying her prayers. An iron chain stretched between them and the prison officials.

Then they saw him come stepping down the stairs. Stately and good-looking. "Exactly like my son!" thought the mothers who had sons. Holding a piece of paper in his hand, Good-looking moved toward the chain. What next, how did all happen? One mother stepped quietly up to Good-looking and took hold of his arm. "My dear child," she began and started to say something. Good-looking pushed her back. "I'll … in your mouth," he said. He pushed her again. The mother fell. As she dropped to the ground, she began to wail and weep. "Oh my son, my son, my son, he's dying in there. So this is where I'll die. You can get rid of my corpse but not me while I'm still alive."

Words were flung back and forth across the chain, from this side to that.

"Did you bear this bastard crop? They're all from the same batch of rotten seeds."

The response came quickly:

"You were never even a seed. You didn't have a father."

The headscarfed woman blushed, embarrassed. Never in her life had she heard such vulgar words. From every side she was offended and hurt. "Oh God, if only I were dead. I'd be better off dead." She hated seeing this filthy row drag on. Stepping forward, she came up to Good-looking but was shouted down before she could open her mouth.

"Get away from me, whore."

"Oh, my boy," she said, " Oh, my boy. I'd give my life for a memory like yours. Your mother and I were in the same line of work when we were young. How well you remember!"

She hated herself for saying it. Her shame was so deep that she wanted the earth to split open and let her fall in. She turned and left, making her way back to the far end of the line, where she collapsed. She weighed the words that had come out of her mouth against herself as a person. They didn't suit her at all. She sat stock-still, her mind a blank. After a few moments she asked herself, "What if I hadn't answered him back, what if I had taken that word away with me, carried it in my heart until I died? You couldn't have, woman! Your heart wouldn't have allowed it in, woman. That would've been a dishonor!"

She now understood the other mothers who had answered the officer with their curses. Obviously they came from places where cursing was accepted as normal. The way they behaved didn't clash with their past lives.

Then she assessed herself. "It was bad what I did, it was bad,"she said, laughing. But not such a terrible badness. God knows, behaving dishonorably is a less forgivable sin."

15.

YES, WE CAN SPEAK

Next the mothers lost their names. Alberto's mother, Tiko's mother, or Dolores's mother is how they came to be summoned. To be called by their sons' and daughters' names they happily endured this one loss.

A loose relationship bound them together. For many years now those who had been meeting on visitation days would drop their variety of casual or more serious friendships and pick up the next week where they'd left off. On other days each one involved herself in that other life, outside.

So how was it between the sons? This remains foggy, there's no way to know or tell. Not enough to go on. The mothers, for the most part, appear to be travelers in this new city not built for them, from which they've been excluded. On days fixed for visiting and court hearings they come together at designated locations, then they scatter. Setting off in every direction.

You may blame a daunting weariness for this. But this is a fact: people can't easily embrace relationships that open up in their lives before an actual need for them has arisen. Only when a deep-rooted cause exists are they allowed to bond in relationships imposed on them by external circumstances.

It was the hunger that created this cause.

It was the hunger that blew away that tent of established habits.

What shall we *do*? What *can* we do? *What* do we do? This is what they kept asking each other. They were on common ground for the first time, under the awful threat of a fire that had to be extinguished. The kids have set off down the route of hunger. The kids are going through with it. The kids are resolute. Death seems to have become the kids' passion. They'll die, they'll die.

"Come on, let's go," the quietest one among them cried out. The one who had to travel the longest distance to the city. "Come on, don't wait. Let's go beat on their doors."

They joined together. On that day, for the first time, the mothers, grouped together like cranes on migration with tired, drooping wings and feathers, made their way down the sides of the main streets. On and on they went until they had gathered timidly before the great doors. To stick close together. To take center stage. Or to hold back fearfully. They placed all their trust in a few mothers from the city who were best able to put their words together properly. "Let *them* talk," they said.

And for the first few days, it was they who spoke. Their names were taken down, like a concealed threat. They were shouted at openly. Subjected to intimidation. But on occasion, there were hopeful signs of goodwill.

On their third march it happened. One of the spokeswomen let loose. "That's it for me! From now on I'm not going to speak for anyone else. Every one of you can say what I'm saying. What we're going through, what we want to see happen, the way we speak to each other about all those things, that's what we should be saying and how we should talk to them."

She shoved the shy ones forward. And stared them down. "Come on, it's your turn now, then it'll be yours."

At last one of them got angry, both at herself and at the others. "Hey, man, come on, don't we have tongues too? Why did God put one in our mouths?"

After straightening up their headscarves, these new spokeswomen got down to business. They did their work well, taking plenty of time to speak their piece. When they stepped back down the crowd greeted them with smiles and chuckles. "Good thing you were so shy! Good thing you were at such a loss for words!"

16.

Rejection

He tore up his verses by the hundreds
Took his name out of circulation
Blotted from his heart those words
Taking the form of poetry

You who adore your own bodies
Who are in love with your own light
You who lie asleep in your own warmth
Snug in your comforter, the night,
What is this? What?

As a youth he was only a poet
Who wrote but didn't wish to touch you
He thought you weren't worth touching
He rejected his lovely poems
He rejected you

17.

Smile at Me Again

Where we'd once lived. In a so-called apartment on a street lined with masses of ash-colored blocks. We were on the ground floor. With a room that opened onto a little balcony. Our household was one of working parents and schoolchildren. Gripped by barren subsistence, we, like the apartments, could only grow dark and gray. In a life spent scurrying back and forth no room was left for flowers.

You had planted some climbing vines. Huge beanstalks sprouted. They went winding around the iron bars on the window. All through that summer they kept their bright green color.

Do you remember? You were still small. You nursed stray puppies you'd picked up off the street. They grew so well and so fast no one would have imagined they were motherless. You and your sisters made your-selves their parents.

When you were taken in, you asked for some seeds. So you could grow flowers in your cell. Despair, futility, none of that mattered. You grew them anyway.

And you told us about a snake. It stayed with you for two years. Or was it longer? You shared your milk with it. Made friends with it. Never let it out of your sight. Later, when I heard no more about it, I took it that something had happened to the snake. I asked one of your friends who'd been released. He explained. There were rules. Snakes were forbidden. You'd wrung a promise from them that it wouldn't be killed. What then? No one can know, not you, nor your friend, nor I.

So then, bereft of flowers and snake, with your hands on your knees and your eyes fixed on the facing wall, enduring a life of idleness, speaking not a word to anyone, how did you ever survive those long days? Remember. You took journeys in your mind. Went any place you liked, saw any-one you liked. Took up the life you yearned for right then and there. You formed relationships and broke them off. You fulfilled all your soul's wishes.

You set yourself free. You had greater freedom than you'd had outside. Endless, uninterrupted, boundless freedom.

That's what you'd told me. And I believed it. Had trust in your strength and stamina. This son of mine won't be beaten down.

And that's what I'm thinking now. My son won't be beaten down. Were the loves in your life before lesser ones, is it because you're in there that your feelings have grown so deeply rooted, why are you so passion-stricken this time? "Like the friend who wounds the rose."

He's a brave one, he can stand pain, can take anything denied him, he can only be shaken by passion. Then, just as snow or ice do when exposed to heat, he melts.

You went quiet for months. For months your face wouldn't brighten up. You never laughed, never smiled. Didn't eat or drink. You said in your letter, "I'm no longer alive." I melted away with you. I died too. But not for a moment did I lose the belief I had in you. A breeze will spring up, a rain shower will come to take away the hurt in your heart. No, I didn't say that. I couldn't say that. What I said was that a day would come when that gen-erous heart of yours would embrace its passion also. As it did your suffer-ings. And it would become a part of you. But would stay quiet and no longer trouble you. You'd gather up all that you'd scattered about. You'd fashion a face fit for your face and a body fit for your body. You'd be your-self as you should be, and you'd smile at me again.

Didn't I tell you?

Didn't I say I knew my son.

18.

IN THE LAW COURT

"The plaintiffs have been brought in." Clad in gray prison uniforms and with clean-shaven heads, they took their seats. The impression they gave was of patients edging on recovery following a serious illness. Every one of them. Autumn leaves set to be whisked away on the first gust of wind. Thin, exhausted, pale. Hardly even able to move. Whereas before this they couldn't sit still or miss out on the chance to turn and smile at their families, now they sit with their heads bowed. No longer even noticing what's going on. The only remaining link is the one that binds them to death. Their life-line could snap at any moment.

The rows of seats are filled with mothers, wives, husbands and other close relations. The hearing charts its own course, proceeding with the minutes, witness testimonies and intermediate rulings. The plaintiffs and their families remain detached. They have no interest at all in what occurs in this hearing. The plaintiffs are focusing on the formal criminal complaint they'll present. After struggling to rise, they attempt to stay on their feet long enough to explain their situation in a few words. Why they embarked on their death fast and are now tendering this criminal complaint. In a few sentences they explain the mistreatment they've been suffering in jail and submit their complaints about those responsible for leading them on to their death fast. They want this put down on the court record. That is their one and only point of interest.

"Complaints denied."

The families are only concerned about the health of their sons and daughters. How can they be kept from starving to death? Some have brought little packets of candy. A few were lucky enough to get them over to their kids, husbands or wives. They feel happy. As if they thought a few sweets could last for years.

One mother has a special interest in this. She's sat quietly through these hearings, year after year, slipping out quietly near the end, always timid and respectful. This time she has a few packets of toffee with her. She sits up near the front. Alert, anticipating those moments when attention is directed elsewhere, to get the packets to her son. But hoping in vain.

Standing nearby was the guard who had brought in the plaintiffs. With his kind face. It was obvious from the way he behaved that his heart held an essential touch of humanity. As he watches the youngsters his face fills with pity. The mother looked at him intently. With his help she'd deliver the packets of sweets, no bigger than the palm of her hand.

The hearing ended. She moved toward the door where those being held would exit. She reached out her hand. Tried a few words to say what she wanted. The guard was horrified to be addressed directly in such a way. With everyone looking on, judges, lawyers, the whole lot. "No," he said. "I can't do that." The stark contrast between that soft, humane countenance and the words uttered by his mouth infuriated the mother. This mother who for so many years had never been angry, hadn't let anger into her mind, this patient, quiet mother. Who couldn't conceal the rage in her heart. Before the prosecutor, the judges, the lawyers, the youngsters, their families, she cried out. "Don't let them have any. They shouldn't eat a thing. They should die. Let them die. Death isn't only for them. Everyone will die, everyone. Why don't you know that, why pretend that you don't?" Her voice echoed in the courtroom. Her ringing words made her braver. She said it all again, everything she'd said, then all she could've never said before, and more.

In that hearing room where even a fly's wings could've been heard, the ruling judicial powers—they who were there to frown, to reprimand, to punish—sat still as stone, their faces suddenly become white as sheets. Not saying a word. The mother saw that the utter contempt for life displayed by these youngsters now ruled over the whole room, from the panel of judges sitting at the bench, to those accused, to the witnesses and the audience, who all appeared to be bound together. And that between herself and those she had never spoken to, met, or seen—those judicial authorities she would never see outside this court room—a pact or understanding of some kind had been established.

If they'd wanted, they could've let fly at her a thunderous shower of reprimands. If they'd wanted they could've had her thrown out of the court. If they'd wanted they could've taken her into custody for showing disrespect. Not one of those things happened. Once all she'd harbored in her heart had been freed in one breath, no matter how brokenly expressed, the mother felt light. She left the courtroom. There, at the doors, as she crossed from one over to another, they who were enshrined forever on their high post remained blanched, turned to stone.

Because that's how the moment was engraved in the memory of the mother, never to leave her.

19.

Dear God, may they who deny healing themselves not mend
Dear God, may these days be gone never more to return
And smother us before a swelling breeze can arise

20.

BLIGHT

From the outskirts of Sansayama, the eastern city of many gates, and from villages far and near, they came. It wasn't the imprisonment of their sons, daughters or daughters-in-law that drew those thirteen mothers together. It may not have even been the hunger strike. Because the mothers didn't quite understand what had been happening. They couldn't have understood. The world had to penetrate so many layers of cloakings and taboos before it could reach them. They had always stayed silent, had always been weak, always submissive. Lords of the land, their overlords, fathers, husbands, sons... Could they have ever reached the world, have ever made it through all those layers? It was on that side of those folds and layers, in their partly visible constructed world of wood and wire fencing, that they had first opened their eyes. That's all they'd ever known. Nothing else.

The men, now...they'd go out. And they'd return bearing signs of the other world on their clothes, in their looks, in their manners and on their tongues—on their tongues especially. The women were left spellbound by the tales they told. Females came into those stories too, with their hair, their lips, their clothes, their money, their demands. With names and titles, and with men who bowed down to them, may God help us.

Then one day the alphabet, along with notebooks, pencils, schools, teachers and writing, reached them. Spanning those layers. If only for show, girls and boys stood side by side. On equal footing. The race was on. Lots of things started happening. Folds and layers started to fray, to wear through. To grow threadbare, beyond repair. Tattered, ready to fall to pieces.

The mothers felt uneasy. A brutal wind from outside was blowing through every rip and tear. They had no one but God to watch over and forgive them. He alone could be trusted. Lately, however, something had happened to him too. Couldn't he see or hear? Why wasn't he fixing the things that were falling apart? Couldn't the mothers go on living as they always had, snug in their sheltered nooks?

No, they couldn't.

The gale that had whisked their sons and daughters off to the prisons was raging too hard to be turned from and ignored. It swept them up. Bore them away to see how their sons, daughters and daughters-in-law were faring. They went each week or two. And they learned about orders, iron bars, and force.

Their first link to the outside world was forged by guns, death and blood. That was their introduction. They were educated through pain.

For so many years, on so many occasions, they came to the city walls, entering through a gate in the wall. For so many years they squatted beside walls made of stone and cement, before the iron gates. So many times they came to line up with IDs in their hands. Their names were called out. From afar they saw their sons. They weren't so very different from the mothers of prisoners in other cities. But for one thing: how poor, how desperately poor, these mothers were. To find such poverty as this, we'd need to go back to an age before our age, and to one before that, before the times of leather, nylon and plastic, all the way back to the iron age and the stone age.

Most of them walked barefoot. These feet had never met rawhide or plastic. Should I swear to this? How else get you to believe that their feet were naked.

As they de-boarded the train from the east at the capital city's railway station they were still bound to their poverty. The feet of two of them yet remained bare. Winter was turning toward spring. The others had at least managed to find some old shoes to wear. But the feet of these two were still entirely exposed.

The prison in the eastern city was infamous. Even birds gave it a wide berth. Rumors spread. Were whispered from ear to ear. As the repression, torture, beatings and cruelty became unbearable, death fasts had begun. With each passing day the inmates weakened more. And were carried off to the hospital. Over the headboards of some perched death. An early death.

It was then that the mothers had united. Had taken their petitions in hand. Had somehow scraped up the means to board the train. Had got in touch with people they knew there. Friends who'd come to the station to meet them.

The mothers de-boarded at the station of the capital city. And walked and walked and walked. Never once thinking about their heads, their backs, or their feet. I can't say they were like "space" creatures, because we've been trained to imagine space people as wearing ultramodern outfits. No, they were more like creatures from the backwaters of time.

As they went on and on, the mute found their tongue, the voiceless found their voice. Those who'd never cried out in anger shouted loudly.

"Come and help us, our sons and daughters are dying."

Why did God stay silent? This was something he could never, ever let pass. He must be waiting for just the right time, one humans couldn't know of. But for the mothers time had run out, none was left. God said nothing. The big doors stayed closed. Those in authority remained silent. The mothers were bounced from door to door like a ball.

On the second day already death announced itself by telegram. Death, may blight strike you and turn you black.

The sons and daughters-in-law of both barefoot women had died. Then others, more sons. Like crops still green. Yunus, the poet, saw into those whose hearts had been seared so.

The mothers left, taking back not only their bodies but their ashes. Having risen up to cross over all those folds and layers, and after finally reaching that fairytale world of dreams, they got more than they'd bargained for. They went back. And while they went, they left an offering behind them.

As they made their way along, they took rage, rancor and incalculable pain, mixed them together, and planted them all up and down the roadsides, right where the soil and the cement met.

BLIGHT.

Will these structures with seeds of blight creeping into their foundations ever thrive?

The blight will rot them. There'll come a day.

21.

On the Front Beyond Justice

These words don't really suit you, son.

Oh, yes. It's been many years now. You can't look out at the sunrise or the sunset, and you can't see the star-filled sky. You only take two steps in that place before you run out of room. You're suffering a punishment without conviction or sentencing, and that defies all reason. Punishment, not only in concept but in point of fact, can be expended. That's how it's known, how it's written in the laws. Anyone who has or hasn't studied law will see it that way. How wrong! Real punishment is what's not in those laws. It's what's not taught in law schools. Punishment isn't expended, it's made to breed. It increases itself on its own, needing no one's help to grow and multiply.

An example? Whoever had those socks knitted and given to you to wear surely had the right intentions. No one can doubt the good intentions of officialdom. Nor should they be doubted. You people didn't want to use them. Why? Because they'd be impossible to wear. Because they'd be horribly sweaty. On top of that, you argued, wearing those socks all year round was not in the rules.

Take heed and remember this for good. Those for whom the rules are made will be seen to have fallen astray of those rules the moment they start speaking of them, and even more so if they want to seek refuge in the rules. This is because only those with the right to make rules have the right to refer to them. If you had stayed quiet back then and done as you were told, you wouldn't be having all this grief. And now there's a rumor that you got in the trouble you're in today by "clamming up." Naturally. For a silent person too becomes a source of unease. Breeds anger. I mean, what did you hope to gain by staying silent? Did you want to show how patient you were? Several times a day (if what they say is true), you were served up with palm cudgeling. That didn't change a thing. You got manhandled and shoved around. No change. You got thrashed even more. Still no change. But they're human too. Which is to say that they can get nervous. Which is to say that they can get fed up. Truth be told, anyone put in their place would react just the same. Would react in just such a way against such a refusal to react.

Or to say it another way, from any angle we look at it, all of you are in the wrong. You want proof of your wrongfulness? It's as clear as can be. The very fact that you all happen to be there, in that place.

I'm getting on, son, just look how scattered my words are getting. Oh dear, now what was I saying?

The moment you refused to use those socks, you went astray of the rules. What means did they use when you kept within the rules? Clubs, shoving around, cudgeling and such... (There's a whole inventory of other humiliating acts, but let's pass over those.) So...you wouldn't expect them to apply the same methods to those who acted outside the rules, would you? More effective ones had to be found, of course. But you can't say that these methods were imported. They set the dogs on you? Never mind the lineage of those dogs! They were raised on our one-hundred-percent homegrown produce. So you can't say that they weren't brought up and looked after well. We observed them day after day with our own eyes. You people are just making things up at the hearing. And getting them recorded in the minutes. Anyway, would those little bits of flesh ripped from your palms or cheeks really be enough to nourish those dogs?

As for your bloodied laundry, the honorable official put that point to rest quite well. "Come on, now, you mothers, you're just like your sons. If that were your sons' blood, it would not have been allowed out."

Anyway, you had to be persuaded. And so you were." Then why not just give it a rest? Why go on and on about the rules? Your talking just breeds more punishment. In every way, shape and form.

Then, silly me, I come to visit, but of course not, visits are forbidden. Or how can I hope to see you when you're so thin and shrunken that you'd only curl into a ball and drop under the counter.

Punishment, as I said, is bred from itself. It increases itself until it finally grows beyond you. There, on one side of the punishment and left unmentioned in the law books, is the family. Us. Those who have the right to come for visits. I'm not counting the betrothed, loved ones and others. They're not thought worthy of having any part at all in the terms of the punishment. They can never come to visit. We must feel happy that we have the right to be accepted into punishment's embrace.

After staying inside that place for so many years, a person needs to know all these things. And thereby know where to stand.

22.

Opened and Reviewed

They knew those we desired
Reviewed all that we fancied, what we craved
Which mountains we smashed in our anger
Which rivers we gazed down on in grief
Reviewed
Our greetings and barbs

Deep inside us, deep
Down in the seas, in grief-stricken lakes
We bear a longing, we rub it
Each night we make it shine
Without a stamp without a sign

23.

In Passion

They've set him apart. In a place under siege. They've taken him inside walls within walls, filled with wire fences, iron bars and locks. Might he be three steps from the farthest wall? One day he'll prevail against all those windowless walls, those cement courtyards, those narrow corridors, the iron bars. He has no doubt about that. No matter how many years go by, he'll be up to it.

One thing he can't bear. A life without passion. Hunger, thirst, sleeplessness, he can do without these. He's proved it. But he can't exist without passion. That's the one problem he has with himself and still can't solve. If the other end of his passion has no life, he knows this end he's on will rot and fall apart. He must be able to keep the other end alive too.

Passion was given to him. From outside. Once upon a time. This is the most precious gift, or more truly the most vital one, he ever received. Do they want to take that away now? Do they want to withdraw that from him so he'll cool down? That's the one thing he won't stand for. Passion must be preserved. Even if it costs him his life.

Intuitively he sees destruction looming. He sees that what he can't touch, what he can't reach right off, is fading away. Nobody can help him. Only he himself can do that. How to stop the deluge descending on him? How to keep it from sweeping that most precious thing away? Passion, however, is looking for excuses to fade away. It wants to take away, one by one, all the loves he's stored up. His feelings for a close relation, a comrade-in-arms, a brother or sister, a friend. Such hopeless cases he can endure. He passes on his loves. He counts them for nothing. At first bit by bit, then the whole lot. He meticulously rubs out his mother and father. With great care erases his friends. He nourishes passion with all he's given up. But passion, just as gigantic, always wants more and more, lots more heads. Until there's only him left.

He agrees to all that. He sacrifices everything and is left with no bonds. The game isn't played in secret. It could never be played that way. He takes up all the painful sounds made by his close relations and friends and hands them over to passion. Passion screams out its triumph.

He doesn't want to see anyone. So he sees no one. He writes to no one. And he forbids anyone to write him. Just look at him there, all on his own. With no protection or defense. Face to face with passion, and one inside the other. At times passion reaches out to him from its outpost of retreat, only to complain, to ask for more, to broadcast signals of despair. Let it stay there. And be just enough not to disappear.

One day, left with nothing of interest or no other life to offer, he offers up his own soul. The soul neither eats nor drinks nor sleeps. Seared by tobacco. Thin, wasted.

On some days passion doesn't broadcast its signals of hopelessness. Days when it shows its face in greetings or news. Once he's seized onto this lure, he doesn't drop it but runs with it for a long time. He scatters flowers along the roads he hopes he'll be passing down. It's this aspect of the game, this turning to face hope, and beholding it, that brings him back to life. Whether dying or undying, he's made it this far. He'll go even farther.

24.

Autumn Photos

Things eternally in the making somewhere
Are stirring
Some done, remain fixed in place
Waiting to be painted or photographed
Or so we imagine
On one side of autumn that faience stove
With its blue, fleeting hues
On the other side rain
If that's an iron cooking stove
In the winter kitchen
Set and photographed
It can't sit quietly
It will be watching
As all at once they come
Smashing themselves against walls
It will be watching
That gang of tattoo birds
Beaks, wings, all blood-soaked

And the I love you picture
Why aren't you in it, I've forgotten
You've cast yourself from the frame
Like a bullet fired into our skies
Returning as only yourself, no frills or extras
That's how the I love you picture survives

Chilled by the cool evenings, not that one
The other
Lying behind it
How I'm old and broken, how'll I mend myself
And how manage to hide out in the cracks
No one should see, I'll rip it to bits

Do what I may, it's just no good, not ever
I can't make my own better

The Hunt

You were three years old then. We were living in A., between the mosque and the prison, in a lodge assigned to us. It was a single-story place, with a great, huge living room and hallway and two side rooms facing each other. Down at the far end across from the main entrance was the kitchen. It was the end of summer when we arrived there, and in the evenings we'd get chilly. There were you, your sister and me. For us, the best place in the world was our kitchen. It was there that we spent most of our time. During the day the big stove for cooking simmered quietly, but in the evenings we'd really stoke up the flames. Was that stove our fourth family member? No. It had to be the first, because we couldn't have lived without it.

Do you remember how the narrow kitchen door opened out to the unkempt, weed-covered back yard, hinting of autumn, with a single pear tree right in the middle? The back-yard walls had been torn down. A few people who passed by cut through the garden so they could reach up and nip a pear. Any of us who witnessed this fruit-snatching would call out, "Your eye gives you the right, so you have to take it." You two would often sneak out to play in the garden. Then you'd come back inside to have your bread and butter or yogurt sprinkled with sugar, and a bit of fruit.

The town was high up. On a plateau where dark fell in the early evening. The dark made us all three uneasy. There in the kitchen, on the kilim and the cushions, we'd sit waiting. I told you tales that no one else in the world had ever heard. "That's really funny," you'd say. Your little one-and-a-half-year-old sister echoed "That's really funny!" And we'd all laugh. So our uneasiness left us. We'd wait for father to return. At times for as long as three dark nights. Then after a few days and nights, usually at the least-expected moment, we'd see him come in. But just before, we'd hear his voice intermingled with the sound of his car or his horse. "Whoopee!" He'd set out for the villages. And from the villages he'd return. And thus we waited. We three. On those days and evenings when he wasn't in the villages, something would boil up in all three of us. It wasn't tension. Nor was it excitement. Not only joy or anything else. But a mixture of all these. It was expecting something to happen that had never before or would never again happen to us, something that we'd experience for the first time. Just the three of us. How lonely we felt.

There were people around. We had neighbors. And there was Aysel.

You couldn't say your *r*'s then. Don't even try to deny it. I've got proof. Aysel would bring along her little boy, Zafer, and you all played together. You both called him "Zafey." Little Zafey had a mind of his own and couldn't be kept home. When he came by, winter or summer, never mind, you'd all three rush out to play.

Aysel used to tell me of her life. She was young, well-built and blonde. An immigrant from Thrace who had got accustomed to Anatolia.

When it snowed, it would go on for days. All the roads would be wiped out. Before the freeze set in, men dug ditches from door to door. Then, taking their guns, which they called "Temel," meaning "basis," they set out to hunt. They were after hare. At the age of three you'd run off with them and come back home in the evenings half frozen, slingshot in hand. As we sat in front of the stove you'd regale us with exciting tales about the hunt.

"So where's the game?" we asked teasingly. "I didn't shoot them, I didn't shoot them!" you'd cry out. "I just took them in my hands, cuddled them some, and then let them go."

Later, in the days after you'd started middle school in another town, one of your teachers, the one who liked you most, would say, "He's just like a young roe, taking off and leaping over one wall after another." You lived a life of boundless freedom, doing as you pleased, with an endearing way of getting around anything forbidden, so that they didn't have the heart to "curb" or punish you, she used to tell me.

Were you really a big brown-eyed roe, and why, lacking any basis, were you hunted down?

26.

We speak with the same tongue
We don't speak the same language

71

SATAN

He stands facing us. His face oval, black hair a bit wavy, an expression that conveys a variety of shades like that of Christ on the cross. His clothes have been chosen carefully enough but to do no more than leave us with an impression of casualness in keeping with his well-shaped figure. He's now become the image of a latter-day saint. Considering how naturally he adopts those airs, it could very well be said that he's made maximum use of it in the past.

I've known him since my twenties. He's gifted enough to play the Satan if that's what he wants. We've met often on some business matters, in certain official capacities and duties. More accurately, on those occasions we confronted each other..

His profession had been chosen for him at birth. Along with everything else that he might enjoy having. The young girl he married looked as if she'd been married for a thousand years. When they stood together as a couple, it seemed they'd been married for a thousand years. When they produced children it was as if they'd never had any. Everything was ordered and planned out for them. His daughter's face looked like that of his wife, just as pale and lifeless. Faces that saved you the trouble of granting any meaning to them. His son looked somewhat like him but a lot taller and wider...ugh!

"If he likes he can play the Satan." That's what I've said, but not just out of the blue. I've actually seen him operate in that capacity twice, flaunting power and authority each time. In one case he was the director of a professional organization. In his tastefully arranged office filled with antique-glossed furniture, he was scolding a friend of his, not much younger than himself yet one who had entered the profession late and who wasn't well off. Digging his new shoes into the carpet, he let fly a mouthful of sharp words:

"How could you do this? You began your internship declaring that you weren't working anywhere else. We made inquiries and found that, in fact, you were. I'm curious to see what you'll have to write in your defense."

If it hadn't been for that mocking last sentence, the intern colleague would have explained the situation right then and there. That, in fact, was the purpose of the visit. The intern would have said, "In fact when I made my initial declaration I was not working anywhere else. It was only two months ago that I was driven by financial necessity to take on a job. In a few days my internship will end."

But those words were never uttered. The intern said nothing at all. Just left the room in a shiver and with a brow that felt as if it had been touched by the demon's own hand. Burning all bridges with the profession just a few days before the end of the internship, and not offering a word of defense.

The intern had seen through the person who would head the inquiry — not to pass judgment but to wound — and couldn't face a future that had been determined by a hellish demon. Forgetting the internship, the profession and any sort of future, the intern said, "Let him wait. He'll have to wait a long time to hear my defense."

It's a shame that our paths were destined to cross. Unavoidably. Each time we met, his Satan's face had grown a bit thinner. I also saw him when he was director of a highly respectable institution. I watched from afar as he entered politics and rose in power. I didn't have to meet him then, for I stood apart from politics.

Nowadays, his articles and declarations appear in the press. He speaks as if the country's justice and laws are in *his* possession. An unquestioned authority. And actually his words are quite good. The visage of Christ on the cross lies behind his writings.

He's now taken his place on the staircase, on the third step up. He hasn't let anybody in, he'll be dismissing his audience from where he stands. He's listening to the mothers. I'm in the crowd too but standing off to one side. I'm there to observe but saying nothing, hoping to remain unnoticed by him. He's into his role now. Throughout the sad and sorrowful narratives his crucifix look grows more intense. Making the most of a gentle and humane attitude, he tries to explain that he has no authority. There's nothing to be done, he won't be of any assistance.

Doña Maria, a teacher who has a way with words, speaks out:

"How can you speak this way? I don't believe you can be so powerless. There's much that the Opposition can do in life today. At least one can voice some criticism, ask questions. Are you going to let all these young people in critical condition, who are about to die of hunger, count for nothing? The oppression and torture they've gone through, will you count those for nothing too? Will you just be watching them die? Some of those kids might have been close relatives of yours, could have been your own children. Put yourself in our shoes."

At that he loses his cool. His face turns deep red in anger. Any significant hint of Christ on the cross vanishes from his eyes and his words. The Satan I've known all along comes out and takes possession of his face and body:

"How can you even *dare* to mention my children? How can you compare my children with those, the ones inside? God forbid! My children would never, could never be like them.

He is on the verge of spitting into the air and touching wood to shield his kids from evil eyes. He's forgotten all about playing the Opposition. Revealed his true nature, haughty and majestic.

The mothers stand there amazed, taken completely by surprise. They turn to look at one another. "Are we talking to the wrong person? How can that be? His name in the book of honor for so many years. To be trusted and praised. Taken to be on our side."

"In the eyes of God," says teacher Maria, "can such discrimination exist among human beings? Have you got a title-deed for God too? So that he can work for you, so that your kids won't suffer like ours?"

Slowly we make our way out. And so we disperse. Never before had we been, and never could we be more silent, mournful, broken.

28.

THE DRAWING BOY AND THE POET

Your tawny head that leans just so
Over the ponies you draw quietly
I take them with me
Hundreds of Pegasuses above the city

In your harbor the silvery sprinkles
Left by the rowing boat's rabbit paws
My words reach out to wipe them, wipe them off

Your brownish-gray shepherds in their winter clothes
I take them to the Ionian Sea
Thyme in one hand olive in the other

74

The flight of birds you hung over the Genoese painting
You loved so much, I dare not touch

Then over your picture's surface you draw a fog
Gun barrels, barbed wire, death, uniforms
Heart in my mouth, my hand won't reach out
My tongue mute, my words broken

29.

EPIC OF THE UNENDING NIGHT

Walking around and around, I've left midnight way behind me. Crashed out, exhausted. Morning won't come. Leaning my head on my arm. Morning won't come. Struck down like an animal. My wound doesn't concern me. It wouldn't matter to me if I died. But in the trap I'm caught in I can't move. Morning won't come.

They took her away. During the day. From her work. "If you only tell us," they said, "if you say where, if you turn this one over to us, we'll let you go. If not...". Morning won't come.

My wife, my lovely, hardworking, clever wife. My warmth, my refuge, my honeycomb. My boys' mother. Morning won't come.

"She knows nothing, she really doesn't. She only does her job, works hard, is devoted, productive." I must've dropped off, my own voice wakes me up. Morning won't come.

My boys, our sons. They're asleep, ignorant of the world. I covered them up, brushed their brows with my lips. How will I ever tell them? If they were to ask for the truth, if they asked, "Where's mom gone?" Morning won't come.

"One taken away to find someone else." But how can that be? How would we know, how *could* we? Who was it? What had been done? "It's you who should be thinking about that. If you only hand over who we want...". Morning won't come.

I must have dozed off again, lay down with all my clothes on. The door bell starts ringing relentlessly. I guessed right. They've brought her back, brought her back.

She shoots me a quick look. As if lost to us, cut off from home. In and out of the rooms they go. What are they searching for? Who are they after? Why? I don't know, I have no idea. Morning won't come.

My wife, my lovely, my stranger. Did that glance of hers hold a hint of reproach? Why reproach? All this is out of my hands. How could I get you out of that outlandish spot you're in now, and back here to our home?

It's like she's a stranger. To the cloth she spread out herself. To the kilim she's standing on, to the bookshelves she'd neatened up. She only looks around. Lost to the objects around her, outside the world. Someone watching from the other side. As if she'd taken on the distant airs of those who've brought her. She doesn't ask after her sons: "How are they?"

Our boys. They're sleeping. Morning won't come.

Some pictures of us are on the wall. With our eyes, our hands. Curious photos. "Who's this? Who're they, who, who, who?" they keep asking. Indeed, who were they? They've been up there so long. With us for so long. In our home, in our living room. So much a part of us. And now we're supposed to see them in a way opposite of that, with different eyes. How could we do that? I can't. Morning won't come.

My wife wanders through the rooms. Now here, now there. Like a sleepwalker. Along with those who brought her. As if she were seeing the books, the pictures, the photos for the first time.

Just before she goes out, she looks once more at me.

A violet torn from the stem. Its purple battered. The yellow centre brooding. From her half-open lips comes a scatter of words. Only one, just one. Is that asking too much?

If she said, "I'm fine," if she asked, "Did the little one have his milk?" or "Were they cheerful when they got home from school?"

She doesn't ask.

My name that she spoke a thousand times a day. Now meaningless. They take her away again.

Morning won't come.

....

Night doesn't end. The ringing and ringing of the doorbell woke me up. Doors opened and closed. People coming in, going out, knocking things over, setting them back up, clumsy feet, clumsy hands. Who could they be? I can tell one door from another by their sounds: the hall door, the kitchen door, the living room doors, those of the study, the bedrooms. They never stop going in and out of the rooms. They're in my mom and dad's bedroom now. I hear the creak of the wardrobe opening. Deep voices mixed in with my mother's. My mother's! But didn't she go on a trip? Didn't my dad say that? What's happening?

Night doesn't end. My brother lies sleeping. Breathing deeply. His lips half open. Quietly I got up. Opened the door. Lights on in the room opposite. Some men. Between them my mother. Her coat on. They ask questions. She answers. The men point. Look around. What are they looking for? I don't get it. I'm scared. Good thing my brother's asleep. One goes out on the balcony. Now others go. I shut our door quietly. Listen to their voices. I'm afraid. Where's dad? Why, why did he allow them to come in? Is it midnight? Cupboards being opened and closed. The harsh grating of the metal bedstead. My mother's angry voice. "Nothing," she says. "I don't know," she says. "How should I know!" Night doesn't end.

They're at our door. "Quietly," says someone. "Please," says my mother. They come in. I'm scared. I pull the quilt over my head. My brother sleeps on. Good. He'd be scared. I'm scared too.

It's my dad. He comes up to us and listens. To our breathing. I'm taking even breaths, pretending to be sound asleep.

They go out. I sense my mother. A step behind them. A little pause. The closing door. A quick look at us.

Night doesn't end. The rooms, the living room, empty. A tired silence hangs over our home again. My dad is trying to hold back his cough. The sound of footsteps. He steps back in. Right toward my bed. Beside me now.

"All right," he says. "Come on, quit playing around, you're not sleeping."

I move a little. He bends over and kisses me. I hug him. "You're a man," he says. "You're a big guy of eleven. You can't be frightened. Your mother and the others came in...". "I know, dad," I said. "But why?" "I don't know either. Let's just hope it won't be long, that she'll come home soon. Your brother's still little. He wouldn't understand. So don't tell him. Let's just keep this between us. Man to man. Let him think his mom's off on a trip. Anyway, look. It might not be such a long wait."

"Okay."

My brother giggles. In his dream. If I could only color his dream with my crayons. I do that. But the night beats down hard. So the colors don't stick. My red, my blue, my orange don't stick.

Night doesn't end.

30.

Separation, floating waterlily,
Can be seen, can't be held.

31.

AHMET BEY

He spent his last night talking in his sleep about a friend. Endlessly.

"Ladywife, Muammer is here, why don't you let him in. Not there, here. That's more comfortable. My dear man, take a seat. Ayşe, dear, come on, some coffee for Muammer, I can't take any..." His voice fades out. "No sugar?" he murmurs slowly. Must be asking himself. No matter from how far away a friend comes, he knows how he takes his coffee. So how could he have forgotten?

For so many years now he's been a native of the mountains and the forests, with his wife and kids, a few men, and the odd peasant who turns up for business or happens to be passing by.

When a friend from his youth stops in for a visit, he fusses over him, going out of his way to make him comfortable. Takes him over to the Istranca Mountains, to Çamlıköy where Tekirdağ opens out to the Black Sea. There, two streams flow into a cove on the seashore, forming a little lake. With water lilies. He unties his boat and rows his friend over to the water lilies.

"Are you a bee, a bee-bird, or a butterfly?" asks the water lily. She can't figure out what they might really be because they seem to be lighter than either a bee-bird or a butterfly She allows them to enter her green and flowery bed and rocks them there until day arises.

So let the morning come... With the daybreak Ahmet Bey brings snow down from Akçadağ. And if that doesn't quench the heat, he takes his friend to Göktepe, with its cool earth and supremely blue sky. They lie down on the grass under the pines. If they wish, they allow themselves to slide gently down the hill to the edge of the deep creek. You can't stand up there, for the creek sucks you down. They fix their eyes on Gökyar, the deep blue creek, all the way to Gökırmak. Only in that spot on the upper heights can you view eagles' nests and the few pines and wild pear trees that droop from the cliff as if they could come crashing down at any moment. Bells, the voices of shepherds. But goats are silent, they creep quietly up toward the herbs and flowers they want. Nothing now but the tick ticking of their hooves.

"Ayşe, dear, gather some mushrooms, light up the cooker. Why are you late this morning? Don't you know we've got a guest? Let's grill some mushrooms."

"Let's take Muammer Bey..." —for some reason this time adding the respectful "Bey" to his friend's name—"to the Bey mountains. The Yörüks are there, Yörük bread, butter-fried eggs, honey..."

Then for a time he falls silent. He's tired. Might his consciousness be pressing onto him the fact that winter began in a hospital room in the city? That he's been going back there more frequently? That as new symptoms arise he feels ever more exhausted?

Opening his eyes just a little, he directs his gaze on everything white in the room. His heart pushes it back, way, way back to the snowy mountains. "It's only there that white is beautiful. Endless... Where God is endless."

"Ayşe."

"Yes, father."

Ayşe calls him "father." Ahmet Bey understands. Because like everyone else his daughter-in-law Ayşe always calls him "Ahmet Bey." So do his wife, his sons and his daughter. Ahmet Bey of the great big world.

"What d'you think, am I going to die?"

"No," says a weak, weepy voice. "You won't die."

"Let's you and I go and see my son once more. It's been months since I saw him. Before I die. Just once. He can't come to see me. Behind bars, locked doors, locked up. Prison. Sons can't even come to see their dead fathers. So how am I to die? Where are my sons to hold up my coffin? I want my sons."

"We've got our daughter, Ahmet Bey. You have your daughter."

"Yes," he says, closing his eyes. He picks up his daughter, calls his sons to his side. They're just starting to grow up.

"So, where shall we go today?"

"Let's go to the seaside." Is it the youngest one saying that?

"Between Gerze and Alaçam, where the mountain stretches out toward the sea...I'm flying, all over the white. Hold my hands tight. You're a big girl now, you can fly on your own. My boys...I have to take them to the guest house at Alaçam. If only I could. The smell of pines, of seaweed and fish, the sun. He has to fly up to the sun, the blue sky has to fill up his breath. He has to swim. Could he? He's been lying in bed for four years now, indoors. Could he swim? What if he sinks...Oh God! What if he drowns?"

"What's with this bleeding now? Just when we're dealing with the blocked arteries."

"Stress."

No matter what the doctors say, Ahmet Bey is flying, holding hands with his boys, one on each side. "Why am I not happy?" Ahmet Bey inhales deeply as he flies over the trees and the sea, but he can't draw in the smell of pine and seaweed.

"Have I made a mistake? Where?"

Consciousness returns. They're all there—his wife, daughter and Ayşe—right at his bedside.

"Ayşe, you should know how much I love you. With the love my son feels for you. It's good, your being here. So good! You're the light shining inside me. If I get better... one day...

He falls unconscious.

Ahmet Bey is dying. "I'll have to take Ayşe along with me. Ayşe who's pining away. Only in her twenties, but always keeping watch over her beloved, always, and so kind... she's my girl. In fact all his sons, his daughters... Every one of them. Of what use are the water lilies? And what good are the birds? So much sun, so much light, I've gathered so much from the mountains... If I haven't passed those on to..."

"The young people..."

Ahmet Bey died. An ordinary event, one could say. I don't know if it was announced in the papers... One of our veteran foresters... As death comes to all. Young or old, famous or fameless.

Death for some might mean life being covered over with earth for all eternity, but Ahmet Bey will keep right on going. In a pine sapling planted and looked after, in the water lilies on the lake, in the red hare that ran away in the nick of time, in the portion of blue assigned to the world by Gökyar, in Ayşe's heart, in the drawings made by a sensitive son.

In you, little boy, in you, and in your son too.

The Blonde Girl

She was waiting with everyone else at the door. As the time approached the women and younger girls who had been sitting and talking in scattered groups of twos and threes began to slip quietly up toward the front. The chatting cooled down and all socializing was disrupted. Because the hour was drawing near. The hour was singular. As was the door. And what most truly mattered was the singleness of the one who would pass through that door.

Across from them, at the other door, were the men.

It suddenly occurred to her to wonder why, what did the separation mean? These are the women, those are the men. She thought of other kinds of separation as well.

Life had turned toward absolute separation, dividing up instead of bringing people together and embracing them all. This was certain. An absolute certainty.

Right on the dot the door opened. The official shouted out: "You will enter one by one." One by one six of them went in. The seventh had the door shut in her face. The six who made up the first group were almost always the same women. Over the years their skill and alertness had reached a height that was beyond question. So much so that, for almost a year now, if it happened that one of them didn't appear in the first group of six—an extraordinary situation, quite obviously—no other woman would dare approach to take her place. The woman had disappeared into the ground, perhaps. Or had donned the robe of invisibility. And when the time came would reappear. Reassume her visibility.

While it was not difficult for the rest to accept this as a fact, nevertheless on assessing the situation they found they were in a dilemma. Inwardly they were respectful of the others' ease and alertness, yet after the first six women had gone in they had no qualms about talking behind their back.

"It's selfish of them. They don't know how to behave in public. They have no respect."

It seemed that those left behind were appraising their own behavior in view of the first six.

"Sure, the ones at the back weren't all that alert and attentive, yet they were behaving without thinking only of themselves. They were respectful. They knew a thing or two about manners."

Every time they gathered at the door, each time they queued up to enter and arrived at the same conclusion, their own self-vindication, that is, they sensed how baseless such views were. But they did not dwell on this feeling. Or, more to the point, they could not. They just let it go.

Being skillful, bold and alert was one thing, selflessness, respectfulness was something else.. Why had such virtues fallen apart from one another? Why had they become associated with faults rather than virtues?

Those women who stood at the door kept talking and thinking in the same the same worn phrases until that slim, blonde girl began to mix with them. Was she the sister of one of the inmates, who had travelled there from somewhere far away? Was she a wife in hardship? Or one of those released?

She never acted as though she were in a hurry. She never argued with anyone, never wrangled over her turn. They thought she didn't know any better. "Just wait till she sees how things really are, she'll learn the ropes soon enough," they said.

She didn't adjust, nor did she bare her teeth to snatch a place in line. But neither did she look stupid. She behaved in a casual way, joining in conversation and offering her opinions.

When informed of their reaction to the six women in the first group, she said, "It's they who interest you, so you don't see the others, because the time we spend waiting for the door to open is longer. Naturally, it's those up front who attract all the attention. Then there's the fact that we, the crowd, feel lazy about pursuing a thought, so we give up on it. If you'd take a look at the second group of six, you'd see that they don't behave at all differently from the first six. They separate from each other, so that each becomes only one person in the line. And we can't forget that with so many people crowded together, that's bound to make a difference too. Everybody goes through the open door with the same consciousness, not looking back, even once. Even if there's no difference between us and them, with them there's no looking back, no hesitation, no thought of those left behind."

"And what about us?"

"Is there an 'us'?" asked the slim, blonde girl. "Does an 'us' exist? Can an 'us' emerge from those who are divided, separated, singled out? We are no longer 'us.' We are one, two, three, four, five, six. The tenth one, the fifteenth one. One by one, at two o'clock, we enter through one of two doors.

Each one of us stops for five minutes at place no. 3, or place no. 8, speaking in words pre-arranged and cleansed of any blame, and then returns. We're warned against speaking of 'our sons,' 'our daughters.' We are told, 'You must say, "my son," "my daughter." This is what's wanted and expected from us, and this is what's presented to us."

—How true, how very true.

Such approval was expected by the blonde girl. She accepted it. Yet what she really wanted was not their approval but for them to go on thinking and expanding on the idea. For now there was no hope of going any deeper.

She wanted them to understand that each of them was one among many, yet each was a human being. That only if they all passed through that narrow door, keeping one another in their hearts and minds, never forgetting or pushing anyone back out, never putting off thinking about them all—only then would they consciously be able to sustain their human dignity. She wanted them never to put off looking back, and to keep their eyes on what had happened way back, long, long ago, in the struggle for human dignity—to trace the path back through history and to see our age, our present time, for themselves. And to comprehend the meaning of what was happening right now. Why those inside *are* inside. Why those outside *are* outside. And why we are at this door and the men at the other door. They should grasp that. Then no one will be anxious about falling behind, because the fight is to get rid of both the door and its keeper.

Slim, blonde, calm. Not a derwish nor a saint. Lost in thought, she suddenly woke up to find herself standing all alone at the door.

She scolded herself: "And you, what about you? If you let your thoughts breed, bringing about nothing for the day, what would they call you? As the poet once said, 'Oh the remedy you claim to be that's not true remedy.'"

33.

TOO TIGHT TO FIT

That we burn inside like embers on ash inside
That we burn on quietly
For whom is that reproach meant

That in our bosom we feed a fire
Great enough to destroy the world
Who knows who can ever know

If there in those huge spaces
If we could sit there
If we could sit where it's too tight to fit
Mothers
A day is on the way
Who knows who can ever say

34.

THE LAST VISIT

All hope for them had run out. What was going through these kids' minds, what were they up to? This would be the end of us all.

—They'll die. No matter, let them be fed, what good will it do after such long hunger? Their limbs are going numb, their arms, their cells dying. Irreparably. They'll be crippled for life.

—What if they collapse when they try to stand on their feet. What if they hit their heads.

—It's already started. They say that some had a brain hemorrhage when they fell.

One of the women was a doctor. A mother or an elder sister?

—Once the base-to-acid balance is lost they'll be brain-dead. There's no turning back.

Mothers, fathers, sisters, brothers. They were dying as well. All life was being sucked from them, just as it was from those inside who had collapsed at the last hearing and were borne away as light as birds, their skin stuck on their bones. Transparent. No longer even pale. Hands cold.

Most of them were now allowed visitation. As if their term of punishment were over and done.

Two women, both mothers, had been keeping themselves calm and composed since the start of the hunger. They had even called on everyone else to steel their nerves. "Let's not give the ones responsible for all this any reason for joy. Let's behave with dignity. It's what our children would want from us. Let's not bring them more sorrow, let's not offend them."

A group of mothers were taken in, the rest, holding their breath, waited. How would the others come out?

All of them, every one, came out crying. Some desperate, beating their breasts. One was flailing on the ground. "He's dying, he's dying." No other words. A young official held her by the arms, gently, trying to seat her on the bench and soothe her. Some other officials stood by the door giggling: "Why bother? Leave her alone. Let her cry."

One of the mothers struggled wildly, pointing to a man's large watch on her wrist.

— "Wear this, never take it off," my son said. "Never come here again," my son said. "You'll never see me again," said my son.

She was drowning in her sobs.

"Long live death! Damn torture!" she shouted. They cut her visit short, she crawled out. My son my son my son. He'll die. They'll all die.

The second group's turn came around. The two mothers, calm, collected, like trim, unburnt candles, were staring downwards or at each other. They had no more strength to move their lips.

They went in. Number one...number two...number three... They stood side by side. Across from them were their sons. One was on his feet, as his hands weren't tied behind his back he held on to something, leaning his head on the wall as if he were just coming out of a drunken stupor, hardly able to open his mouth, his tongue in a twist, his broken words rising with great pain.

—Don't be sorry, mum. Don't cry. Stay the way you are. You're my mum, think of that. Get my fiancée some violets for me. No one should cry. Death would come anyway, so what if it comes a few days before or a few years later.

His mother opened her mouth. Unable to find her voice, she closed her lips helplessly. With her eyes fixed on her son, she begged him in silence.

The mother beside her looked around for a while. At first she couldn't see her son. Then, after a while, she made out his head down below. Was he sitting or bending down? It was her son's head. How could it be there? He couldn't stand up straight. Not a single word. For a minute he held up his hands. His fingernails were all purple.

His mother lunged desperately to grab hold of the iron bar, else she'd fall. The iron bar, so solidly, so officially built into the wall, came off in her hand, losing her balance she staggered backwards. Her body crashed against the wall at the narrow corridor's far end.

When did the visit end, how did they get out of there, neither of them could remember. The mothers who had gone in with them were too embarrassed to cry . They said it would shame the other two. But those two were hardly able to make it to the courtyard. Weeping, weeping, they flung themselves down beside the flower beds.

35.

The gallows are set up
Death is at our doorstep
Echo our voice, no matter how low
If you keep silent
You're dead already or on death's side

36.

HAIL THE MIGHTY PRESS!

Why is this waiting lounge so cold? Because it's facing the exit? I touch the radiator, it's like ice. Shivering all over, we wrap up in our scarves and shawls. For more than an hour we've sat perched by the door in scattered rows. When two of the mothers took off their shoes and tucked up their legs, they looked just like the winter birds huddled on branches, trying to protect themselves against the cold, their feathers all ruffled up in a ball. Don Pedro and father Ernesto seem sorry to have joined us, as if, being men, they'd been stamped with an indignity.

What will happen? What's to be done? What *can* be done?

It was no coincidence that we all converged at the gate of this state authority holding a petition with one hundred and eighty signatures, each with a stamp on it. We'd got the word that "Apple" was calling a press conference. The government spokesman Romero Oblitas had got the nickname Apple because of his plump, red cheeks. Less than six months had passed since he'd won the votes of the majority, even though he was no different from the others. We already knew that. So?

So, why "so"? So, busy as bees, we gathered up hope like specks of yellow dust. And there we were, clutching at the tiniest hints of it. Is there anything else we could've done after our sons and daughters were locked up by unfeeling hands? Hope. It so happened that there were ways to overcome deaths, illnesses and the endless captivity that lay ahead. But how could such ways be employed by this sort of mixed band of people too wary or scared to speak of their troubles openly or look for help? Out of hundreds of mothers and fathers only one hundred and eighty had finally signed the petition, and only five of us took part in its delivery.

The young people meant nothing, and, as their close kin, we were expected to adopt the same attitude. What we said, whomever we visited, all was under surveillance, we were forced to take back every step we took as the siege around us tightened. We were all subject to constant intimidation, so that, in that very spirit of counting our children for nothing, we would have to let them weather their fate alone.

We were mothers, witnesses to the sufferings of our sons and daughters. The hand raised against them came down on us too. As if our husbands, other children, other relationships didn't matter at all, almost everyone had withdrawn everything else from her life to rebuild it on such pain as this was. Obsessive and stubborn. If we'd only had the courage we should've had! We haven't reached that point yet.

The press corps had just begun to arrive, when the five of us, petition in hand, went up the stairs of the huge building, crossed the entrance and came to a stop in front of the officials' desk. We were asked kindly to state our identity and the purpose of our visit. We said we wanted to see the Respected Apple, that is Romero Oblitas, and that we were the parents of the jailed ones. If it had been any other day, we couldn't have even crossed through the gate outside. But here we were, standing at the entrance, which was busy with the press people, clutching our several-metres-long papers made of the strung-together petitions.

"No," said the official, it would not at all be possible for us to see Apple—Romero Oblitas, that is. "We watch the Respected Apple—Oblitas, that is—on television. His full-length pictures are posted all over, those of his respected wife and of his son and daughter are there in the papers too, in swimming suits or fully clothed, at home and at parties, at sea and on land. He's just like another part of us..." we said to the official.

"You'll have to make do with that," the official replied. "The Respected Oblitas is a man of the people. If he's a man of the people, then he's a man who's got to be seen by all the people all at once. What would become of our democracy if we set you above the others?"

"Fine," I said. What we really want is not to see him but to speak to him. To report to him our complaint that can't be put off."

"But everyone's got troubles," the official replied. "This morning my wife was crying because she'd run out of gambling money, that I had to bump up her allowance, her dressmaker has died so who'll sew her clothes, her daughter was dumped by her boyfriend and ruined all hope of marriage, as a mother what was she supposed to do about all that? Now, could I possibly load all this onto my boss? He's got his problems too. We've all got our problems, lady."

The press crowd around us was getting larger, keeping track of our conversation. The official had started to sweat but we were resolute, our faces a fortress wall. All at once we saw the one skipping down the marble stairs inside, approaching us hastily. Since he didn't have any questions for us, the matter must have already been reported to him. A higher official, polished, affable, suave. He laid hold of our petitions and soothed us when we didn't want to hand them over.

"I promise you, I shall take this up to him at once. There's a press conference now, so he won't be able to receive you. But he will read your petitions and do whatever is necessary. Believe me." And so we believed him. What else could we do? Our petitions were now in his hands, he took them away, with all their one hundred and eighty signatures. Two of the journalists took copies of them.

For a while we stood lingering there as everyone else went in. Something was missing, something we hadn't managed to pull off. We could sense that. What we had done, was it going to end up as it usually did— an attempt with no immediate consequence? "Let's go," said one. I could see that Don Pedro, father Ernesto and the other mothers were about to take off. "There's something missing in all this, something left undone ," I yelled out. "Yes, I think so too," mother Marselina replied. "Something's missing, but what?", and Doña Maria went along with that. "Isn't there anything else we can do?" I asked, walking on the left and followed by the others into that cold and senseless emptiness that was called a waiting room. Then we sat on both sides of the door, slumping idly in our chairs, and waited there for an hour. Confused. Undecided. Bored. Tired. Feeling cold.

I was thinking. The press people had come in singly, but on their way out they'd all be together. Could we? Possibly? Just get up and say "Stop." Doña Maria, her eyes lit up, said "Yes." The others couldn't make up their minds. The two of us, all aflourish, like water in a cistern struck suddenly by a light, rushed out under the bright blue winter sky. The others hung back at the bottom of the stairs. When the crowd exited the press conference and began to make their way down the stairs, "Stop," we directed. "Listen, hear us out. There are things we have to tell you, how could we find you otherwise?"

They stopped. Every one of them. Not one walked away. Just like that, we mothers kept them there. Reported on what was happening. Not a word more or less. We went on to tell them how angry we were, and rebuked them for closing their eyes to the perilous incidents that any day now would lead to deaths. For not doing their duty. Doña Maria let them know what was going on inside—all the torment and torture.

Not a sound came from the crowd. When we had nothing left to say and started to walk off, a good number of them came over to draw us into their midst and ask questions. To our horror we discovered that in their eyes our case was just one among the many that had become routine to them. Now they seemed to be coming out of a stupor. To have seen the light. They swore that they would pick up the case, now, straightaway, and get through to the necessary places.

And as I took a last look at their faces, I believed their words in my heart. The other mothers and fathers did too. The mighty press—the eyes, ears and voice of a mighty country.

This time as we walked past the gardens, we felt fearless under the blue winter sky. Right before our eyes the trees sprouted leaves. An apricot tree was about to come into flower. Daffodils and lilies were in bloom. The ever-blooming honeysuckle perfumed the air around us.

We looked at one another with sparkling eyes. "Right," we said, "Now nothing's missing."

37.

JUAN AND PEDRO ALMONTE'S MOTHER

We're having a long summer lasting through the autumn months. And we're all five of us enjoying it, Julio, Carlos, I and the two policewomen, Amanda and Rosa. Well, who wouldn't, having to watch a prison gate, being stuck inside the unplastered walls of a jerry-built structure, its old chair and desk, the window that doesn't shut right, especially after going through this last winter! We used to burn the stove but it gave off smoke. When we opened the windows, the fumes were no sooner gone than the fire went out too.

Miss Amanda and Miss Rosa, both from the political police, sit side by side at the table, wearing identical uniforms and with their hair cut short so that they look like twins. They deal with the women who come for visits, frisking them from top to toe, picking through their bags.

Yesterday a lady lawyer came in. After searching her Amanda asked, "You do have a mirror, don't you, or didn't I see one?" The lawyer was taken aback. Was this her first time or something? "Why?" she asked. "Not allowed," said Amanda. "Mirrors, tweezers, keys and such. Ohhh, yes, no newspapers either." The lawyer was obviously new here, because she still had a mind to question, whereas all the others had long ago got used to the procedure and did as they were told in the blink of an eye. Every one of them. "I don't understand, what harm can there be in a hand mirror or a cupboard key?" Amanda let her have it, "Don't get smart with me, you'll do as you're told." The lawyer lady turned red right up to her crown. So pretty, so attractive! If I hadn't felt shy I'd have said, "Don't you have another question or two, lady? Why not just go ahead and ask?" Both Julio and Carlos agree with me, I can tell from their faces, each of them lost in deep thought. My God! What a figure, those eyes, that blonde hair! She was about to storm out in a fury when Carlos stopped her. "And your ID, Miss?" "Those sharp steps don't become you, lady," I said to myself. Like a lightning flash she handed over her ID, stuck her card on her collar and was gone. Carlos stood there gawking at her photo. And, man, did we wait for her to come back by on the way out!

We sit right on the edge of an endless wood, surrounded on all three sides by green, with a dark gray asphalt road running by out front. The sun is forcing the leaves to let its beams break through and shine on the earth, making the whole world quiver in the fine breeze.

I like the world. I like this room. I like Julio and Carlos. I could even like Miss Amanda and Miss Rosa. Or could've liked them, if it weren't for that elderly lady who'd just appeared in the doorway. She looked like my mother, and something warm stirred inside me. Could've been taken for my dead mother. She came in and stood at Carlos's desk, all weary and worn out, in a wretched state.

"Yes?" said Carlos, frowning as usual. She was my mum, and the warmth inside me was still stirring. "What is it that you want, mum?" I asked as gently as I could, thwarting Carlos's approach. "My sons," the mother replied. "It's been a week since they took them from home. At five in the afternoon. I haven't heard a word from them. It's been a week. I've looked everywhere, knocked on all the doors."

"What are their names?" asked Rosa.

"Juan Almonte, Pedro, Pedro Almonte."

"And you, where are you from?"

"I'm from Gökçam," mum replied. Or some place like that.

"Hmmm," said Amanda. "Your family name sounds somewhat familiar to me. Didn't you have another son, and a daughter-in-law? Carmen was her name, and she used to work in a hospital."

The mother was thrown for a loop by the precise identification, but she quickly bounced back and started to curse her sons and the daughter-in-law. "I wish they were dead, then I'd be done with them." The words came with effort, so she was obviously pretending. But then she added quickly, "I have no idea where that son of mine and his wife are. He was separated from her and I've been away from both of them, it's been a long while since I've seen them.... . Please find my sons for me. I've been on every floor in the police building. They're nowhere to be found. But you, if you wanted to, you could find them."

"Her daughter-in law really gave me a hard time last year," said Rosa. "I was told to go after her. I could never even ask about her at the hospital before she'd find out and escape. They were shielding her, I'm dead sure on that score. For days I was after her, hot on her trail. Since then she's disappeared."

A quick, uncontrollable smile crossed the mother's face.

Rosa was amused. "So why look for your sons if you'd like to be rid of them? Let them be dead and gone."

"My crops need harvesting, I'm all on my own, how can I do all that work myself? I need them. Please, please?" I turned toward Amanda with a look of pleading. "O.K.," said Amanda as she went out to make a call from the commander's office. After a few minutes she returned. "Your sons are with the police," she told the mother. "But don't ask exactly where. Just come back here in forty, forty-five days and look for your sons. This is where they'll end up anyway."

I worried that mum would cry, or shout, or collapse or something. But no such thing happened. "Thank God, they're alive, thank God." She felt relieved to have tracked down her sons. She had found out that they were still alive. Then all at once she got angry. The humble, begging tone had vanished from her voice. She was calling them to account.

"They had jobs in the city, but were sacked. Then they were taken in and held in detention for forty days. Forty days. Of torture. Only God and *I* know how I brought them back to life. Not even six months had gone by. Just when harvesting had to be done. At five in the afternoon. Why? Why? Enough. For God's sake, we've had enough of all this."

"What a family," said Rosa, after mum left. "With sons and a wife like that."

"How about the mother?" said Amanda. "May I be blinded in both eyes if she's any better than her sons. It's just the way these people are."

I didn't like those words. The mother was right. Would *my* mum have acted any differently? But I kept it to myself, didn't dare say a word to Amanda. Not much military service time left. Come on, little walking papers, come to me.

38.

GROW UP

Grow up so from your dad you'll get
Grow up so
Get pains
Grow up so from your dad you'll get
Grow up so
Get noughts
Grow up so from your dad you'll get grow up so
Get endless joblessness hungers
Grow up so
Grow up so from your dad you'll get
Tyrannies tortures
Handcuffs detentions dungeons
Grow up so
When you turn seventeen
Grow up so from your dad you'll get
An execution

39.

No to Growing Up

The little boy lay asleep with his hair spread out like ears of corn across his mother's chest. They were both long-distance travellers. Sitting awake, unblinking, the mother only shifted a little in her seat to keep from disturbing the passenger beside her. It wasn't the boy's weight, that "cherished weight," which tired her out and pained her. Nor was it that dear face, freed from iron bars or cages, lighting up her heart and mind again and again. It was the aimless, meaningless energy drain resulting from their countless travels from the town in the west to the capital city. It was travelling with her boy who had grown to age four as they shuttled back and forth at short intervals over the same roads—from the family home of her husband to that of her parents. Babıla (as the boy called his grandmother) and Eskidede (as he called his grandfather) both wrapped them in infinite love. For the grandparents, their arrival day was the only festive one of their lives, and their day of departure was all mourning, nightmare, murder.

Bending her head over the little boy on her lap, the mother took in his smell—of the moonlit August night, the sea, freshly cut grass. Her eyes filled with tears. "That was wrong, I shouldn't have taken him from them."

Far from the city on the western coast, Babıla and Eskidede had a poor life in their village. Their plot was small, their livlihood mean. When their son went off to university from a free boarding school, they were overjoyed. Even more so when he got his degree, and especially when he married her.

She is almost overcome by sleep. The bus stops for a break, doors open, and she feels better as the air of the summer night happily wafts in. Everybody gets off. "Free teas on the company." She alone remains in her seat, still clutching to her breast her ears of corn. Sound asleep, the child breathes deeply. They had set off from the village on foot. No car or truck in sight. The child quickly tired and had to be carried or held by the hand. "Look where we are...nearly there!"

They couldn't have stayed on in the village with Babıla and Eskidede, who were the kindest people in the world. She had felt they were a burden, adding to the old couple's poverty. And they were too far away from the city where her husband was being held. "Much too far away." So they stayed with her parents in the capital, to rest for a while before travelling on to visit him. Thinking about her parents made her angry. "If only they were like my in-laws, we could always stay with them and not have to worry about how to make ends meet. Would visit him more often too, since they're a lot nearer to him." From the very start they'd been opposed to her marriage. She, from a genteel family! With a peasant! How could she! Then came the days of upheaval, raids, arrests. "Mum and dad, who could be closer? Yet they were so remote to us during those stormy days. All we meant for them was trouble." She felt tight. Having to call on them with her child and stay as long as possible. "If I could work, could get a job and make a living, a tiny house, just for us two, a nest for my little one. Every month we could go and visit his dad. But they're on hunger strike now. What if they carry on with it? Oh God... what if he falls ill, or dies? It's during visitations, that's how our little boy got to know his dad. If he were only released, I'd put my arms around, keep hugging him. And all the rest of them, all, all our friends.—Why, oh why?"

The child moaned in his sleep.

"They took me in the same day they took him. If you don't talk, we'll... In front of him. No, don't, don't. If you touch me I'll kill myself. Premature birth, from extreme fear and worry. They gave up the torturing. Would you like some tea? Why would I ever want to do this to you? I've just got to follow orders."

The mother shifted her weight onto her other leg again. The child awoke, sitting straight up on his mother's lap as she kissed and cuddled him. "Look how nicely you're growing up, and when you've grown some more..."

The boy began to shout, his words loud and clear, filling the whole bus. "I don't want to grow up, all right? Don't want to be a big brother, all right? Don't want to be a dad! DON'T WANT TO GET LOCKED UP!"

Translated by Saliha Paker and Mel Kenne

from *Love is Lasting* (1992)

TWO WAY GYPSY

I'm the silver fox of a long chase
I ran through rivers, I ran in snow
I gave up killing lives are holy
I turned and hunted myself

The lines were ready, gave life to the seeker
They were ready I just retaled the tale

I'm the sun's two-way gypsy, I followed only him
The ways bled with longing, hills rang with my name
I became a tree, my fruit was shaken down, I'm content
My feet walked to my core

I am Hallâc, I am Nesimî, I so believed
I walked out of my skin

Translated by Ruth Christie and İpek Seyalıoğlu

Baroque

Inside every refugee grows a rose tree
Withstanding heat and drought
To have no country is to bestride all countries
Withstanding limitlessness and infinity

It wasn't yearning, no, not sorrow
But resisting yearning and sorrow
As if flung out suddenly with no reason
No law, no code, withstanding innocence

On this baroque body the refugee can place,
With the same elegance, the dreams and the birds,
On one end Vivaldi, on the other Borges
Withstanding crazed masses and sly loneliness

A rose tree grows inside every refugee

Translated by Cemal Demircioğlu, Arzu Eker, Sidney Wade and Mel Kenne

ELEGY FOR THE RIGHT ARM OF MUSA AKBABA FROM LOWER CINBOLAT*

How can I say it, can't get my words right
I struck off my own arm, let go of it
They've pulled my land from under my feet
This cruelty against us, this is death

This one field fed us and clothed us
What is this law, who writes it, who makes it up?
It's a cruelty unknown to the vulture and wolf
My words run short, run out, this is death

Syria's mountains are smoke-veiled, oh my oh me,
What's known as Ceylanpınar is closed to us
Our kids can't race gazelles down to the stream
Let the cranes be the warning to our songs
The lords of Urfa are ferocious

How shall I say it, who's the cause, who's to blame
Never in my life has my fury been
So edgy, as sharp as the blade of a knife
One thing I know, my hand committed the crime
No power is left to me but my own life
What I let fall was mine, my own arm

* "100 acres of land belonging to Musa Akbaba (48) from the village of Cinbolat in the borough of Nusretbey, Urfa, was divided, confiscated and given back to its former owner under the Land and Agriculture Reform Law. Musa Akbaba flew into a fury in the middle of his field and, using a machine for sowing, chopped off his right arm, which he blamed for voting for (…)." From the newspaper *Cumhuriyet*, 16th December, 1987.

Translated by Saliha Paker and Mel Kenne

from *Then I Grew Old* (1995)

SHORT POEM / ONE

—Then I grew old, behold
A sentence as long as a novel

Translated by Saliha Paker and Mel Kenne

SAND

I had a love interest once
who from his hometown mailed me sand
while I was always asking myself
what about its wind
is it soft, is it wild, is it steady?
does it quickly hurl into the skies
whatever it picks up from the ground?

later we took to sharing cities
the wind served as master, I as apprentice
in a rage of coming and going it blew
filling my eyes with sand

Translated by Mel Kenne and Arzu Eker

TRACES

Waiting without a word she was growing old,
in the midst of the humming commotion of things
feeling heavy within she went out in the wind
erasing herself never stopping

ache upon ache as she turned into fire
they opened her up out came words
vicious words, traces of hurtful acts
shades of deception, un-healing forgiveness
out came "I must go," "never to come back again"
"from now it's right in your face
                        everything in my mind"
out came "I must be on my own"
from a secret held deep
an old passion

Translated by Saliha Paker and Mel Kenne

HYMN OF DETAILS

What did I take from whom, from where
I took everything from somewhere
I'm drained, my eiderdowny outside, far away
My patience, granted a lot, I took from inside

words aren't meant to stay, anger you wait
bruised pained pierced, not yet dead
flesh you wait
I must shout, my scream from winter should touch spring
A is forbidden, **no** is scary, I've grown weary of **yes**

Mejnun kicked out of the story – tele-show-
Leyli split into a million copies
copies without any smile, secret, or joke
I thought the smiling masks
were countenances

would I be staying in this grave what's wrong with me
strange, she said, outrageously strange
details, rusty bolts, mossy stones
and what about those underneath those beyond?
Gülten has deceived me.

Translated by Saliha Paker and Mel Kenne

THE HAUNTED MANSION

In that haunted mansion
there with your poems, Emily
a high, ornamented ceiling, six tall windows
snow falls endlessly
on harsh plane trees, soft pines
out back, a half-silhouetted mosque with a double minaret
the sky solely in the grasp of a confused grey
the net curtain falling just over
the old clock-tower's dark shadow
timid, amid newly manufactured things
pushed and shoved aside
shopping markets, foreign clothes, adventurous commodities
warehouses, finally the waterfront facing out
wild quick-stepped waterfront thundering
ready to spill out all it has into the city
and the port, ships from far-off countries
ships from those nearby flying bitter-colored flags
there, in that haunted mansion
with your poems, Emily,
"To wait an hour is long
If love be just beyond "
if love is right there inside you
if you've carried it over
from the earliest moment you remember
in that haunted house
let it go, into the snow, the mist, the shadows
let it go, into worn-down dreams
now's the time for it to slip into infinity

Translated by Saliha Paker and Mel Kenne

DONE WITH THE CITY

Voices closeby gone
nights have changed hands, demolitions
not even mentioned, left tongues
disintegration on the agenda

no one can unite
with the metallic discourse of antennas and satellites
do those who encounter each other
in the midst of foreign names traffic signs alarm bells
really meet? they can't
this is more like a collision
crashing crashing all day crashing
in the city's heavy waters
everyone wounded

men
pricking into their blood alcohol splinters
men being born out of their madness
women
shutting themselves up in their wombs
playing with their secrets

done
with the city

Translated by Cemal Demircioğlu, Arzu Eker and Mel Kenne

from *Silent Back Gardens* (1998)

LEYLA

"you're not Leyla" said Mejnun
the very moment of their union
he was thought to have gone mad

Translated by Saliha Paker and Mel Kenne

THE WHALE

I saw the sky, entranced by possibility, loved the dream
my divings in and out were aimed at "something out there"
how many times, at this thing at that thing
I leapt, got both lost
and marked out
I stayed deep, dove under the craft
I shook
was shaken your strike becoming expert
I went silent fell to dreaming
is the blood yours or from my own wounds
hey captain
I'm no longer the leviathan locked in obstinacy
nor your blue whale

Translated by Saliha Paker and Mel Kenne

CYCLAMEN HYMN

I pushed the door, bravely or foolishly entered
he and the children were the whole world
my loneliness was lost
traded
for a pot of white cyclamen
black kid gloves, colored glass panes
amid a halo of pain
the feared opening up of happinesses,
hidden pleasures
entered my life

a warm look, a denial
into my life came a healthful anger
a slap in the face, my errors confirmed
I offered no self-defense, it was too late
like cheerful apples tumbled out in the open
all I had scrupulously hidden
I stood
stained and bruised right out in the sun

Translated by Saliha Paker and Mel Kenne

106

The Wedding and the Snow

A mere wedding's sadness, warm, diaphanous,
dissipated through the densely falling snow
of the dense silent evening.
So the two saw us off with sweet goodbyes
the little girl, the young woman,
and all the rest were inside
and all along the street
us alone

snow on my chest, you knee-deep in it,
your white wool shawl wrapped around your neck,
we walked.
all the rest were inside, there,
was it that they were foundlings lucky to...
or that winter night, were they so tied
to soft beds in warm rooms
that they found

As the snow grew upon our feet
too heavy then to carry along
were we frozen
trudging uphill
up to the swing-door
where we paused and wept
all in each other

so tranquil, and even softer,
made as though from fine threads of silk
with cheery faces lit by sadness
restrained yet a bit crazy
achybreaky a bit
bringing together the farthest ends, overjoyed,
yet standing so nobly calm

followed by the work of death
is this insurmountable wall now

the type that rises higher with pain,
in the nights of snow to follow
burnt by the yearning,
Alone I kept
walking.

Translated by Önder Otçu

THE SCENE

Is the eye in this happening
the seer or the seen
or has this *I* now become
the whole scene?

Translated by Mel Kenne

THE GIRL WHO DIED ALONE

why does it come back to me now, that girl, her black hair
sleepless as nights without end
in a hospital room
and why was it I whom they placed beside her?

she had hepatitis and a special someone
named Joan
after the letters and phone calls reached her
Salonica, Piraeus, Athens
with the other long sunk into her eternal rest, Joan came

helpless to hold her for a few hours more
in this world, I was embarrassed
they'd closed her eyelids, that deed accomplished
their touch couldn't reach her tears
those Joan kissed

Translated by Mel Kenne and Arzu Eker

from *On a Distant Shore* (2003)

I WOULD HAVE SMILED

I don't like the dark, if it were me
I'd have switched on all the evening lights
I'm looking at the room from the outside, a woman
sitting on the armchair's edge as if about to get up
you've leaned sideways
your face close to hers, your hand on the woman's shoulder
is that me? It's been so long, I've forgotten
here's what the woman says, her head bowed
"I'm tired of you"
had it been me perhaps I couldn't have said that
I might've tendered little smiles
held your hand perhaps
the room is too dark, if it were me
I'd have switched on all the evening lights

Translated by Saliha Paker and Mel Kenne

Nahİt Hanim

Why
did the desk stand so high?
to cow a classful of kids in black uniforms
we didn't shy away from her, from the closed door
she'd pass through silently like a specter
to walk to her spot that would grow quiet
and shrink. We girls breathed freely
her straight, brown hair fell about her face
which was the pale face of a saint
for some it was a mask, never changing
was I the only one to know
if pleasure or grief was there

was she hard of hearing? Or was it
to keep the world's gossip from wounding her.
did she veil herself?
she'd hide her slender figure
under a threadbare old lab coat

from inside her invisible armor
what she said was just right, no more, no less
a few words caught in the air
transported us beyond that lesson

Balzac, Dostoyevsky, Kafka
She brought us from her home, Silone
in the stone courtyard with high walls
I lay in the sun like cats at their leisure
to watch the world

with *Bread and Wine*, the Karamazovs
maybe the *Lily in the Valley*
my dreams grew
who was it who
filled this helpless little girl with such sunshine

Were those rumors "fish in a bottle of *rakı*"
what sort of people were they,
how they spent their evenings I would've liked to know
nights seemed to cover up the day
the class would end, that stork-legged
"Strange Orhan Veli"
in his old light coat, collar up high
would come to take her away

Maybe that's why I laid the blame on him

Translated by Saliha Paker and Mel Kenne

from *Bird Flies, Shadow Stays* (2007)

STAIN

Here we stand at the messiest point of our time

someone should write us, if we don't
who will

the more silence kept, the duller became
the fine knife we used
to carve out raw day

where are they, the flashing miracle
and the shining magic in every motion

one more day unseen
one more day passed withering the grass

so we learn it was blind, as if there were
no alley no passerby
no one to record the passerby

they said
lock them up, leave the key in its old place

but the truth is
it's a shameful thing, as Camus says
to be happy on your own

voices and other voices, where are the world's voices

the stain invaded the tissue
saying nothing saying nothing

Translated by Cemal Demircioğlu, Arzu Eker, Sidney Wade and Mel Kenne

114

GARDEN VINES

It was still the green almond time, we hadn't yet faded
you two little girls would come up
one with big blue-eyed comical looks
the other, quiet, passive

blue pretended to be the world
a breeze of Ulvi Uraz from places of no return
a joy that couldn't fit
into my big-sisterly shell
in the music room fugitive moments
at the window knee-high grass
the back yard

from those days to these
what have you carried over
what have I?

of course in those days too
a few things happened
but Afghan towns
weren't yet a legend
Iraqi children, their mothers...
Iraq in ashes, Iraq in ruins
the Middle East a world wound

As if day no longer exists now
the sky skips over it
nights fall fall into dreams
on the globe some place
a black stain that grows perpetually.
The stain harsh, hurting the onlooker
The one who sees the lesions
Which is why the media
created blindness first of all

from those days to these
what have you carried over
what have I?

Up against the Ziverbey mansion
a house, Istanbul
between roses and screams
I must've been blind, blinded I was then
Outside the sun shone past us

Once the hot frame cools down
it turns really cold
the mouth is shut fast
the eye is no longer an eye

from those days to these
what have you carried over
what have I?

At last the desert dust
Also rained on us
The seas withdrew, the rivers turned yellow
The earth lay to rot

what have you carried over
what have I?

An elderly poet points out root sources
church music, the little boy with the siren voice
wild violets, the Aleppo vines
poplars, olive trees, the wind
the gypsy girl picking wild chicory
The eagle owl
Heavy stones pierced so the water will flow
While all these still exist here…

gülten is all I'm left with, a rose
if ever planted, stranger to any garden

Translated by Saliha Paker and Mel Kenne

SCHEHERAZADE

From a thousand and one inky nights
Scheherazade reached the fairytale's light
voices sheltered by the wind
soared far away upon it

with an arrow inside you trained inward
you stood untrained
you, hunter, who couldn't snag a thing
or else what you took slipping quickly from your hand
you were tested by pain, tested by praise
they saw a likeness, tagged it
"I saw her I saw her," said some
"there was a halo"

what remained you wrapped carefully
buried it in unending night
now everything's fallen away
you're left in mystery, Gülten

Translated by Saliha Paker and Mel Kenne

118

THE CLOAK

"The wind and I are on our own just so"
said the queen
clinging to complaint in sweet consolation
they seemed far away, modern times arrived
where can the crazy queen go to escape?

"deep-voiced, the big, big shoes they don,
hats, faces clean-shaven, anger they don
out they were
the outside–always there,
it belongs to them, we never used it
but were worn out by the time they held the doors open"

the taste of an adventure on her lips
"On my own shoulders I placed the cloak of self- censure"
said the queen
the cloak is too narrow for the frame, for the day,
the unhemmed, the stained, the ripped
taking hazy detours back through time
the crazy queen can mend

Translated by Saliha Paker and Mel Kenne

IN THE PARK I

In the sky a shy, early moon
the city weary of waiting
for market and park to fulfill pleasures
children enter life more masterfully
under fearful eyes
slide, swing, whirl round and round

a woman bursts out laughing
everyone looks, as if they've forgotten laughter
tough guys strut by nudging one another
the city prepares for Monday

homes become more complex
in their smooth-running
grandmas and grandpas are out now
grandchildren need huge spaces
for anger, daily crises,
the small gods' rebukes
their loneliness too, very often

they sob and weep quietly
grandmas, grandpas they're not at home
they'd mend, if they were around,
ageing is losing in a way
to gain they'll die one day

Olga is starting to grow up by herself
Işık takes pains not to do so
smiling teddy bears, sad penguins
mix with the memories of the elderly
in Alaz's voice the swing is set going
back and forth his image keeps swinging

Translated by Saliha Paker and Mel Kenne

120

IN THE PARK II

In each shady spot an elderly woman
counts the passing steps
trying to keep them all in memory
as she strokes the yellow leaf fallen onto her lap
what's in mind scatters
she waits to catch their eyes
whose whose whose whose
children and dogs
talk to me talk to me

Translated by Saliha Paker and Mel Kenne

MOURNING THE DOVE

We both unvoiced the dove
in its usual place the sky
then the day of the lilacs
            of the iris
then roses all through the summer
only she wasn't there
we knew her by the stretch of her neck
by the flutter of her wings

everything was in its place
only she was missing
we both unvoiced the dove
the balcony grew pale

Translated by Saliha Paker and Mel Kenne

LOVE AND LONGING

If I were, if I were a little girl
in the houses that face the sea
if it were to turn up from my dreams
if I could see the white sail
if it wished to come near land, but couldn't
if my shores drew back more and more

that's it!

if I were, if I were a tree
a plum tree grown from the seed
my branches my leaf my flower
if I were pruned, if my owner, master
wished to turn me into an apricot tree
if I were to shout and shout, my voice lost
if not even the wind carried my voice

that's it!

if I were, if I were a young filly at Tayheli
if I reached out touched the harbor
if I let the captive ships loose on the ocean
if I stopped the storm with my whistle
if I woke up with my foot in a hobble

that's it!

near me very near me
I hear the birds perching on your voice
Unless I can touch you you're there, there
if I stretch out my hand, you'll vanish

you're all my longing

Translated by Saliha Paker and Mel Kenne

NOTES TO SOME OF THE POEMS:

ANATOLIAN ELLAS AND THE STATUES:
Ellas (also Elles/Ellez, İlyas) signifies a holy figure in Near-Eastern mythology, symbolizing fertility. In compound form, "Hıdırellez" is an important festival on May 6 celebrating the beginning of spring in the Balkans, in Turkey, and in the Near East. Hızır İlyas in the Alevî-Bektaşî tradition is believed to come to the rescue of people in extreme danger.

RUST:
Çapanoğlu refers to a famous family in Yozgat, involved in an uprising against the forces of Mustafa Kemal during the War of Liberation in the early 1920s.

Two-Way Gypsy:
Hallâc (9th century) and Nesîmî (14th century) were both Alevî-Bektaşî poets. Accused of heresy, Hallâc was cut up into pieces, Nesîmî was skinned alive.

GARDEN VINES:
Ulvi Uraz (1921-1974) A great comedian of the Turkish theater and cinema.

SONG TO AN AGELESS WOMAN:
This poem was written in memory of Behice Boran (1910-1987), a stalwart revolutionary figure, leader of the Turkish Workers' Party (1971-1987), sociologist and academician. She was sentenced to fifteen years in prison after the coup of 1971 but was released three years later upon an amnesty and died in exile in Brussels.

NAHİT HANIM
Nahit Gelenbevi Fıratlı Damar (1909-2002), here referred to by her first name, Nahit, was the legendary lover of the famous poet Orhan Veli Kanık (1914-1950). She had a degree in philosophy but taught literature at the Ankara Girls' High School where she inspired Gülten Akın as well as other students with her passion for poetry and fiction. After Orhan Veli's early death, she re-married and continued to associate with the well-known poets of her time.

AUTHOR AND TRANSLATOR BIOGRAPHIES:

GÜLTEN AKIN was born in 1933. A poet with a unique voice that appeals both to individual sensibilities and a universal social conscience, she was acknowledged as "the greatest living Turkish poet" in 2008. She studied Law at Ankara University and worked as a lawyer and teacher in various parts of Anatolia where she lived and travelled with her husband and children for many years. Her major poetry collections include *Rüzgâr Saati /* Hour of the Wind (1956), *Kestim Kara Saçlarımı /* I Cut My Black Black Hair (1960), *Sığda /* In the Shallows (1964), *Kırmızı Karanfil /* The Red Carnation (1971) , *Maraş'ın ve Ökkeş'in Destanı /* Epic of Maraş and Ökkeş (1972), *Ağıtlar ve Türküler /* Laments and Songs (1976), *Seyran Destanı /* Epic of Seyran (1979), *Ilahiler /* Hymns (1983) *42 Günün Şiirleri / Poems of 42 Days* (1986), *Sevda Kalıcıdır /* Love is Lasting (1991), *Sonra Işte Yaşlandım /* Then I Grew Old (1995), *Sessiz Arka Bahçeler /* Silent Back Gardens (1998), *Uzak Bir Kıyıda /* On a Distant Shore (2003), *Kuş Uçsa Gölge Kalır /* Bird Flies, Shadow Stays (2007), *Celâlîler Destanı /* Epic of the Celâlî (2007), *Deli Kızın Türküsü /* Song of the Crazy Girl (2012). Her critical prose was published in *Şiiri Düzde Kuşatmak /* Besieging Poetry on the Plain (1996) and *Şiir Üzerine Notlar /* Notes on Poetry (1996). Almost all her collections have been awarded prestigious prizes in Turkey, and her work is represented in all national and international anthologies of Turkish literature / poetry; the most recent one of these is *From This Bridge: Contemporary Turkish Women Poets,* by George Messo, published in the UK in 2008. Her poems have also been translated into German, Flemish, Danish, Italian, Bulgarian, Arabic, Polish, Spanish and Hebrew, and used in academic studies. Hilal Sürsal's *Voice of Hope: Turkish Woman Poet Gülten Akın* is an in-depth study of her life and work, published in the USA in 2008. Gülten Akın has five children and many grandchildren, and lives with her husband in Burhaniye, on the northern Aegean coast of Turkey.

RUTH CHRISTIE was born and educated in Scotland, taking a degree in English Language and Literature at the University of St Andrews. She taught English for two years in Turkey and later studied Turkish language and literature at London University. With Saliha Paker she translated *Berji Kristin: Tales from the Garbage Hills,* by Latife Tekin (Marion Boyars 1993), and in collaboration with Richard McKane a selection of the poems of Oktay Rifat (Rockingham Press 1993). Again with Richard McKane she translated a major collection of Nâzim Hikmet's poetry, which was published by Anvil Press in 2002. In 2004 *In the Temple of a Patient God*, her translations from Turkish of the poetry of Bejan Matur, was published by Arc Visible Poets. Recent translations include *Poems of Oktay Rifat*, with Richard McKane (Anvil Press 2007), and *The Shelter Stories*, by Feyyaz Kayacan Fergar (Rockingham Press 2007). In 2012 her translation of Bejan Matur's *How Abraham Betrayed Me* (Arc Visible Poets) was awarded the Poetry Book Society's Recommendation for 2012.

CEMAL DEMIRCİOĞLU works as Assistant Professor of Translation Studies at Okan University, Istanbul, Turkey. He completed his B.A. and M.A. degrees in Modern Turkish Literature at Boğaziçi University, where he worked as lecturer and obtained his PhD in Translation Studies. His main research interests involve the history of translation in Ottoman and modern Turkish society, particularly Ottoman conception/s and practices of translation. His article "Translating Europe: The case of Ahmed Midhat as an Ottoman agent of translation" appeared in *Translation and Agency*, which was published in 2009 by John Benjamins. He has co-translated the poetry of Murathan Mungan, Gülten Akın, Gökçenur Ç., Gonca Özmen, and Birhan Keskin.

ARZU EKER-RODITAKIS has a B.A. in Communication Studies from Istanbul University and an M.A. degree from the Boğaziçi University Department of Translation and Interpreting Studies, where she also began her doctoral studies and gave courses on translation theory, practice and criticism. Her M.A. thesis, *Publishing Translations in the Social Sciences since the 1980s: An Alternative View of Culture Planning in Turkey*, was published by Lambert Academic Publishing in 2010. She currently resides in Greece, where she is working on her doctoral dissertation at Aristotle University of Thessaloniki, on the English translations of Orhan Pamuk's fiction. Since 2007, she has been participating in the Cunda Workshop for Translators of Turkish Literature (CWTTL), where she has collaborated on translations of fiction and poetry into Greek and English.

TALAT S. HALMAN is a professor of Turkish literature and the Dean of Humanities and Letters at Bilkent University in Ankara, Turkey. Formerly, he taught on the faculties of Columbia University, Princeton University, the University of Pennsylvania, and New York University. He has also served as Turkey's Minister of Culture and Ambassador for Cultural Affairs. He has translated numerous books into English and Turkish.

MEL KENNE is a poet and translator who has lived in Istanbul since 1993. He is a founding member of the Cunda Workshop for Translators of Turkish Literature (CWTTL) and has translated much Turkish poetry and prose into English. He and Saliha Paker co-translated the novels *Dear Shameless Death* (*Sevgili Arsız Ölüm*) and *Swords of Ice* (*Buzdan Kılıçlar*), by Turkish author Latife Tekin, both published by Marion Boyers Publishers, in 2001 and 2007 respectively. He also co-edited with Saliha Paker and Amy Spangler *Aeolian Visions / Versions: Modern Classics and New Writing from Turkey, from the Cunda International Workshop for Translators of Turkish Literature, 2006-2012,* forthcoming from Milet Publishing in 2013. Six collections of his poetry have been published, most recently *Take* (Muse-Pie Press 2011), and *Galata'dan / The View from Galata* (Yapı Kredi Publishers 2010), a bilingual collection, in English with Turkish translations by İpek Seyalıoğlu.

NERMIN MENEMENCIOĞLU was born in Istanbul in 1910 and is the great granddaughter of Namık Kemal, the famous Turkish poet and patriot. From the American Girls' College in Istanbul she won a scholarship to Brown University, and went on to Columbia for her M.A. She married Jasper Streater, a highly decorated Royal Air Force officer in the Second World War. During the later 1940s and 1950s, the Streaters' *salon* in Ankara became an essential meeting place for promising poets like Oktay Rifat and Melih Cevdet Anday and painters like Abidin Dino. In 1962 the Streaters moved to London, where she was involved in the Primrose Hill poetry school. Her published works include those in the *Penguin Book of Turkish Verse*. Other works include two large, unpublished tomes of translated Turkish short stories and a biography of Enver Paşa. She died in London in 1994.

ÖNDER OTÇU was born on September 12, 1967 in Ankara, Turkey. He spent five years at Hacettepe University in Ankara, and another five in Oslo, Norway (Universitet i Oslo), studying linguistics and psychoanalytic anthropology. He won *The Milliyet Prize for Literature in 1990* for his essay on *Night* by Bilge Karasu, and he has had critical essays, mainly about Turkish poetry, published in *Adam Sanat* and *Varlık*. His translation of *Selected Poems by Ilhan Berk*, funded by The MacDowell Foundation, was published by Talisman House Publishers in 2004. He has also translated a number of prose works, including (from Norwegian) *Constantinople*, by Thorvald Steen, *Culture Terrorism*, by Thomas Hylland Eriksen, (from Turkish into English), and *Turkey at the Crossroads of the Century*, by Atsuko Toyama. In 2004 his novel *Yağmur* ("rain") was published by Telos, in Istanbul.

SALİHA PAKER is Professor of Translation Studies who retired in 2008 from Boğaziçi University, where she still teaches a course in the PhD Program. Her research in Ottoman literary translation history and other subjects continues to appear in international publications. As a translator of Turkish poetry and fiction, she founded the Cunda International Workshop for Translators of Turkish Literature in 2006 under the sponsorship of the Turkish Ministry of Culture and Boğaziçi University. Her translations include three novels by Latife Tekin: *Berji Kristin Tales from the Garbage Hills* (with Ruth Christie), and *Dear Shameless Death* and *Swords of Ice* (with Mel Kenne), all published by Marion Boyars (1993, 2001, 2007), London / New York. She edited *Ash Divan, Selected Poems of Enis Batur*, which was published by Talisman House Publishers in 2006, and co-edited, with Mel Kenne and Amy Spangler, *Aeolian Visions / Versions: Modern Classics and New Writing from Turkey, from the Cunda International Workshop for Translators of Turkish Literature, 2006-2012*, forthcoming from Milet Publishing in 2013.

DIONIS COFFIN RIGGS (born in Edgartown, Martha's Vineyard, MA. in 1898) was a poet who was also interested in Turkish poetry. She spent more than five years in Turkey with her son-in-law, William Fielder (born in Washington, D.C. in 1924) and lived for a decade in Turkey, studying Turkish with Özcan Yalım and enjoying the friendship of his fellow-poets). Both worked with Özcan Yalım on programs of Turkish poetry given both in Turkish and in English translation at the Turkish-American Institute in Ankara. Some of their translations were later published in the U.S.

İPEK SEYALIOĞLU was born in 1976 in Istanbul and received her M.A. degree in Translation Studies from Boğaziçi University. She attended the Cunda Workshop for Translators of Turkish Literature in 2006. She is a poet and actor as well as an English language instructor at Boğaziçi University.

SIDNEY WADE has published five collections of poems, the most recent of which is *Stroke*, Persea Books, 2008. Her next, *Straits & Narrows*, will be published by Persea in April 2013. Her poems and translations have appeared in a wide variety of journals, including *Poetry*, *The New Yorker*, *Grand Street*, and *The Paris Review*, among others. She translates the poems of Melih Cevdet Anday, Yahya Kemal, and others, from the Turkish. She taught at Istanbul University as a Senior Fulbright Fellow in 1989-90. She is the poetry editor of the literary journal *Subtropics* and has served as President of AWP and Secretary / Treasurer for the American Literary Translators Association, ALTA. Since 1993 she has taught Poetry and Translation workshops in the MFA@FLA Creative Writing Program at the University of Florida.

ÖZCAN OĞUZ YALIM (1931-2001) was a poet, humorist and translator. After graduating from the School of Political Science at Ankara University, he worked briefly as a civil servant. He continued his career as an editor for Elif Kitabevi (Istanbul) and Bilgi Yayınevi (Ankara) publishing houses, and for the poetry magazine, *Yusufçuk*. His poems were published in many of the foremost literary journals of his time, and his humorous stories appeared in several volumes of *Zübük*. While giving private Turkish lessons in Ankara, he met William Fielder and the poet Dionis Riggs, and they collaborated in translating some of his poems and some by Orhan Veli and Gülten Akın, which were later published in literary magazines in the U.S.A. In 1993 he retired to Foça, which is where he lived out the rest of his life.